MYRIAM LAKHDAI

PS: BACK TO YOUR ESSENTIAL HEAVENLY BEING

Or

The Seven Keys Of Wisdom:

"Starting from who you are to become the ideal person you would like to be"

- Novel of Initiation -

OUR 12 ROLES ON EARTH

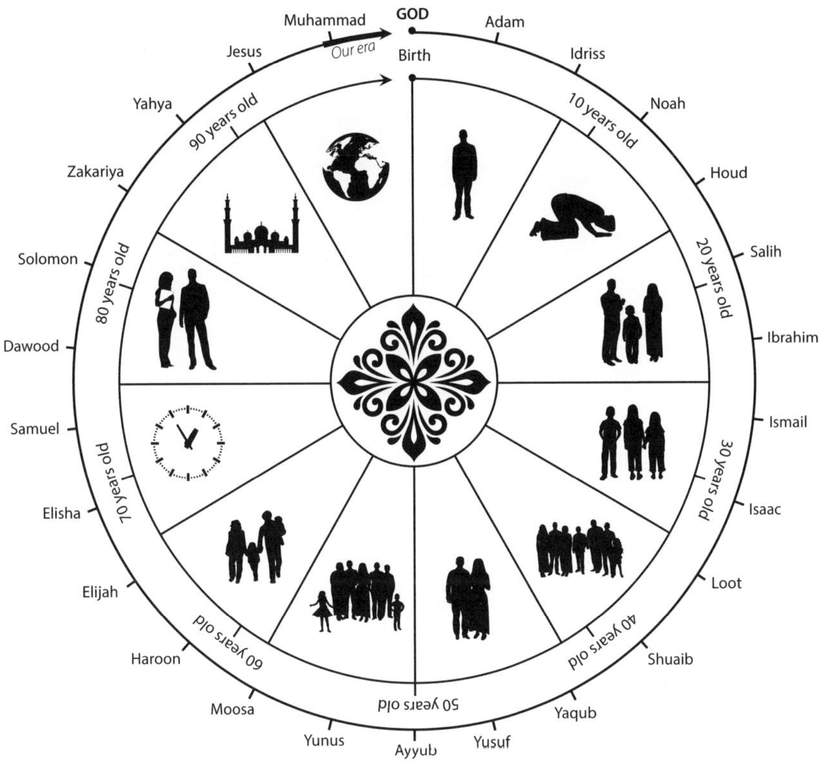

1: Human being
2: Muslim
3: Child of my parents
4: Member of my brotherhood and sisterhood
5: Member of my family
6: Spouse or future spouse
7: Member or future member of my in laws' family
8: Parent or future parent
9: Managing my lifetime
10: As a person involved in a professional life, studies, hobbies
11: Member of my community, my brotherhood and sisterhood in God
12: Member of humanity

BY THE SAME AUTHOR:

- Once upon a time, there was a man and a woman... (Yet to be translated)
- They got married and had many... surprises! (Yet to be translated)
- We will win no matter what (Couple) ... (Yet to be translated)

Come visit our website and participate in our seminars in french
Seminairelakhdar.jimdofree.com
Contact: oumhedi@hotmail.fr / +33 06 50 41 1 04"
Facebook: PS-Back-to-your-essential-heavenly-being

Translation and adaptation from French to English: Akila Chetitah
Cover, design and drawings: Rey of Light Design

DEDICATION

To Hassen and to Khadija, (may they rest in peace).

To my younger brothers and sisters

Samira, Rayane, Mourad, Iliesse.

To my older sister Sakina.

To Ingrid, Rénata, Salima, Hager, Safiyya, Esma

Samia, Nouria, Nassima...

To the sisters who participated to the workshop.

To the sisters of the forum.

To Manoubéa

To the core group Hayette, Marwa, Fatim, Aminata, Ghosna...

To my children Lina and Hédi.

And to all sensitive souls...

FOREWORD

This book guides us above the sensible world, towards the unexploited resources which we treasure within US. This book consists in a **novel of initiation** which will help you reach your objectives by asking you the right questions. It enables you to get to know yourself better and to pave the way for a global change... A rich method to fully make your dreams come true and to fulfil your destiny as the principal actor of your destiny.

This coaching book will follow us, you readers, in the big steps of our lives. It helps us reconnect with the core essentials and with the springs of courage, joy and balance that come from within us. Then, for learning purposes, we are invited at the end of each episode, through practical exercises, to use a notebook, in order to save the teachings read about our own life path.

As a result, the present work offers us actual tools which will help us discover our mission, the one for which we have been created. It also teaches us how to consistently organise ourselves and to direct our activities in a just manner; so many elements which are crucial to the fulfilment of ourselves...

"My Lord, now that everything is quiet
And that in the tranquillity of the night, each lover
joins his beloved, here I am for You.
I stay within Your hands, Ô my Beloved,
Allow my solitude with You, tonight,
To help saving me from the Fire in the afterlife!"

Rabi'a al 'adawiyya

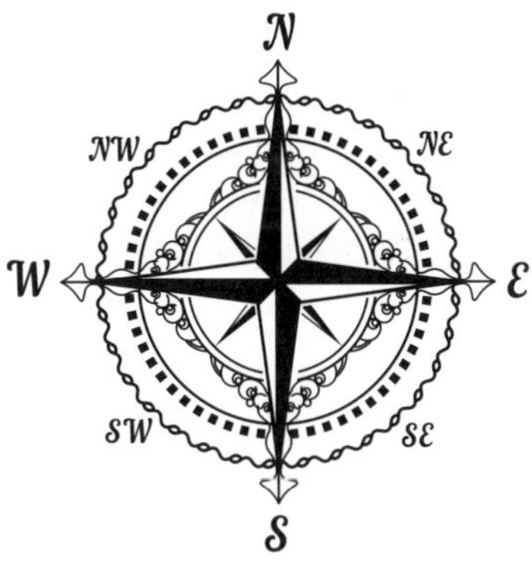

Tools for the expedition within yourself

Your imagination
Your notebook
Coloured pencils or felt pens
A compass = your heart
A bottle of Zam Zam Water
Some dates
A stick = your intellect

"Time loses us

Time embraces us

Time is our train station

Time is our train"

Jacques Prévert

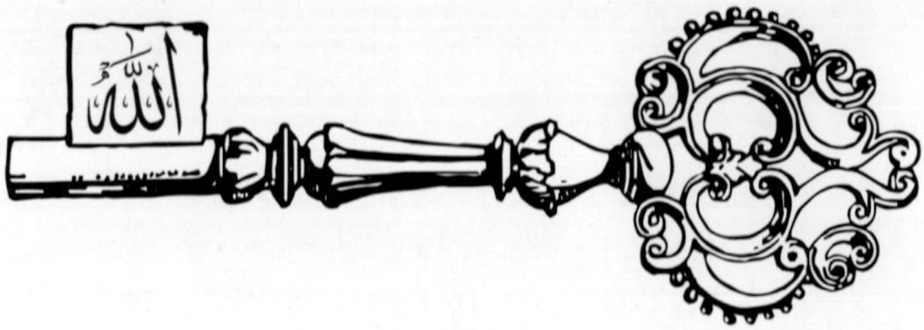

How many of us, on this earth, are trampling on the muddy platform of our day-to-day routine? How many of us are full of negative thoughts, weeping on the edge of our life, paralysed by fear, stuck in our destinies like simple spectators? Sometimes envious or dreaming, but too often desperate, so immobile, far away from God and scared. "I always fail to get on the right train"... said my husband once.

Yet, since the beginning of the year, I noticed in his behaviour a progressive and fundamental change: fasts, organic food, diary, waking up at dawn, going to sleep right after the last prayer. He used to like the delicious dishes of his country, late night stays and sleeping in so much, but now, he reads: the Torah, the Gospels, the Quran, the stories of the Prophets, but also so many biographies of famous men and women. He quoted Muhammad, (Peace and Blessings of God be upon him), Omar, Ali, the forgotten Muslim scholars of history (may God be pleased with them), but also Gandhi, Martin Luther King... No more coffee, not even tea, no more TV either.

Prayers in community, bathing of dead bodies. Always in a state of Wudu, all his senses seemed to participate in his willingness to **give meaning to his life**. He had a thirst for knowledge. He didn't hoard his knowledge, he shared it, offered it without vanity. He was telling me "There are some texts which deeply move me, because of how their echo is in harmony with what fascinates me..."

He surprisingly set as a goal for himself to read one book per day from the encyclopedic book series "Very Short Introductions", that is to say an average of 150 pages per day. It was a means for him, I think, to satisfy his curiosity through learning about different rich and various topics such as Law, Political Sciences, International Relations, Philosophy, History, Geography, Sociology... If he couldn't sit down to read, he would download free audio books, a "Ne'ma" (blessing) for him. It is true, thanks to this, we would discuss, philosophize and listen to the entire works of famous writers and philosophers together, at home as well as in the car, seated or in a busy state. He made me discover *Thus Spoke Zarathustra* by Nietzsche, *Confessions* by Augustine, *Prayer to God* by Voltaire, *Solitude* by Guy de Maupassant, *De Brevitate Vitae* by Seneca, *Tao Te Ching* by Laozi, etc...

He used to love his car and wasn't into sports at all, but he started to walk every day. He said it was helping him to commune with himself. He would take his MP3 Player and wander for hours, wondering about the definition of life and happiness and listening to lecturers such as Mashayekh Sheikhs Tareq Al-Suwaidan, Aaidh Al-Qarni, Mohamed Al 'Adi...

I had never seen anyone who suddenly, from one day to another, was so afraid of wasting his time. I had the feeling that he would do anything. Anything to make up for the time lost. If he could have been able to read in his sleep, he would have done it. He was the one who used to say every morning: "I am fed up with that. I'm always late". Now he was optimising every minute of his life.

Within five years of marital life, he had never been that patient and caring with me. No remarks, no critics, it started generating anxiety in me. Neither my organisation, nor my forgetfulness, not even my lack of clarity were annoying him. Everything which used to work him up, such as traffic jams or my delays, now didn't even disturb him. I could feel he was full of wisdom. I liked it, but it was also worrying me. I even tried to intentionally provoke him to upset him. But he rarely spoke. His words were filled with a mercy which didn't resemble him until today. Not that he used to be a bad boy, but he used to be a perfectionist, he used to say offensive and confusing things. Attention, compassion, empathy. Even his smile had changed. His skin was softer, his hair silky and light, his body was building muscles and was fitter, his gaze was delicate and humble, all of this left me speechless. He became a new man. I had the feeling that, for him, time had stopped.

"What do you think of two, the third of whom is God?"

Al Bukhaari

He had never been as determined as on that Friday evening, in the month of *Rajab**, when he told me: "I want to do *Umra**" (the lesser pilgrimage). It was as if the *Ka'aba** was calling him. As a student, I wasn't working and his salary used to cover our daily expenses. All our savings will be used for it. Yet, as with the reading, he managed to convince me by sharing his excitement with me. I couldn't sleep that night. In fact, our hearts filled with faith, our bodies covered by clothes of light, he could already see us revolving around this building covered with its black and gold *Kiswa**. Hearing him speak about it, I could feel the delicate scent of musk and incense surrounding me. The call for prayer from the holy places was resonating in our bedroom, more than 6,000 km away, we were dreaming with eyes opened.

It didn't take him more than 3 weeks to organize everything. I can still remember his sparkling eyes, when he came in, on that blessed day, with the tickets in his hands. Nobody, nothing could have stopped him. Everything followed naturally, I trusted my inner compass and we flew in the evening to these remote lands. In the plane, the travellers were as excited as us at the thought of making their dream come true.

Even though I was about to perform an act of worship, my faith wasn't hiding enough the fear that I felt when we took off. I felt like a lamb, experiencing the last minutes of its life.

Notes: You will find the definition for the words followed by a star in the glossary, page 186.

All of a sudden, a group of Turkish Sufis started chanting prayers upon the Prophet Muhammad, (peace and blessings be upon him) in unison. Cradled by the sound of their voices, tears of repentance began to run down my cheeks, with confidence. I wasn't able to stop them. Once we flew past the *Miqat**, all the men in the plane put on their *Ihram**.The oldest among them were radiated like candid children, and their eyes were sparkling from liveliness. As for the youngest, they seemed to have accumulated the wisdom of many lives.

Flying on the plane, we had the feeling of being transported on the wings of our most beautiful guardian angels. "Oh Allah! Here we are, answering Your Call! You have no partner. Here we are, answering Your Call! Verily, all praise and blessings are Yours, and all sovereignty! You have no partner!" I was experiencing, with my husband, an intense feeling of fulfilment and communion, at the rhythm of this *Talbiya**.

As light as a feather, the plane safely landed, to our satisfaction; the relieved passengers were exclaiming: "*Al HamdouliLah** wa Allahou Akbar!" "Praise be to God, and God is The Greatest". As soon as the doors of our winged machine opened, we took possession of the ambient air, this new, dry and hot air. Once we were done with the procedures at the airport of Jeddah, we were finally just 50 miles away from Makkah, and we reached there by bus.

Our luggage was taken care of. We then entered, hand in hand, into the holy compound of the *Masjid Al Haram**. I felt over the moon, I couldn't believe what my eyes were seeing. "Me, being here, with my husband, who would have even thought about it? Some 15 hours ago, we were at the other end of the planet". All of a sudden, I understood the wisdom hidden behind my father's words: "Life is a succession of miracles, my dear daughter, never forget it."

Yet, these words aren't strong enough to depict how I was feeling. My eyes couldn't stop staring, contemplating... There is an Indian proverb which says: *"We aren't human beings going through a spiritual experience. But we are spiritual beings going through a human experience."* It is the feeling I had in front of the Ka'aba. I was brought back to the reason for our existence: Spirituality.

As a result, by eliminating all the consecutive layers of our conditioned thoughts and our determined behaviours, by removing, step by step, these obstacles, these worldly desires which isolate us from ourselves and lead us astray from our soul, we finally go back to our initial essence, to our fetal conscience: *the fitra**. It is this state that we reach when we pray together in front of the *Ka'aba*. Therefore, engaged in the mission which was to perform our *Umra*, I followed the directions of my kind-hearted husband. We stayed ten memorable days in Makkah, where a prayer is worth a hundred thousand prayers accomplished elsewhere. After having performed the lesser pilgrimage, we took a bus to the North for more than 250 miles.

Let's go to the radiant city, Medina, where, after two years of preparation and planning, Muhammad, (peace and blessings be upon him), immigrated with his loyal friend Abu Bakr, (may Allah be pleased with him). "My love is automatically given to those who love each other for my sake", said Allah in a *Hadith Qudsi**. In fact, the study of the biography of the Prophet, (peace and blessings upon him), clearly shows us that the way to the right path, in Islam, is through developing and deepening the links of friendship and brotherhood for God's sake. The path of Muslims is the Path of Union, the union of human beings, of the hearts with their Creator. My husband had always been loyal to his friends. He often used to quote Epicurus on this topic, saying: *"Friendship frees from fear and servitude: it is wisdom itself."* Medina was for us, in this sense, the ultimate city of Brotherhood.

Our love for each other was filled with profound respect, because we were aware of the bonds which were connecting us, beyond the bond of marriage. We were brother and sister in humanity, offspring of Adam and Eve (may God be pleased with them), like the seven billion human beings which live on our planet. Then, brother and sister in our faith in God, we had signed another pact of brotherhood by getting married to each other. Our brotherhood in God was even stronger thanks to the brotherhood in humanity which we shared previously.

In fact, remembering the fact that we are first and foremost human beings enabled us to be more understanding towards each other, more patient, more tolerant, more forgiving, more careful and more gentle in our horizontal relationships with our brothers, the human beings, and hopefully, every day more humble and more modest in our transcendental relationship with God. Fundamentally imperfect, we knew how to be so, because we were in constant evolution and "in progress", we had decided, together, to humbly build our future, to build the meaning given to this present life.

The ground floors of the buildings surrounding the Prophet's Mosque, (peace and blessings be upon him), display shops and businesses. The upper floors house pilgrims from all over the world.

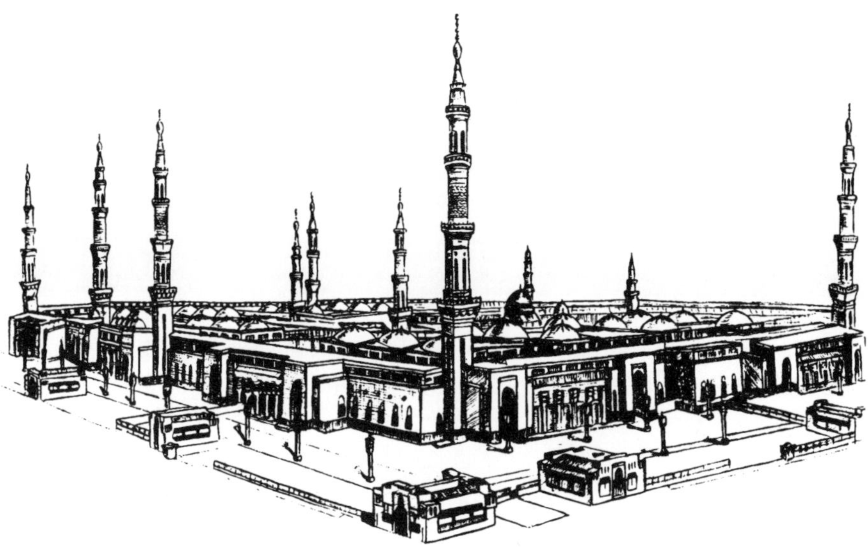

The hotel in which we were hosted in Medina was right above a mall dedicated to incense. My perfumed dream came true. We were sleeping 5 minutes away from the mosque, next to Bab Essalam. From there, we could see, at our arrival, this symbolic green dome which covers the grave of the Prophet, (peace and blessings be upon him), and his two loyal companions, (Abu Bakr and Omar (may God be pleased with them)).

What attracted me and touched me the most in these 160,000 m² with eight minarets, which could gather up to 250,000 worshippers, was this little bit... this little bit of Paradise, this garden called *Rawdah Ash Sharifa* (the honoured garden), located between the ancient house and the *minbar* (pulpit) of the Prophet, (peace and blessings be upon him).

At this time of the year, accessing this garden was a real obstacle course for women. Once there, sisters from all over the world organised themselves. Offspring of Adam and Eve, (may God be pleased with them), one after the other, we would put our forehead on this green mat. I can remember these Indian sisters who brotherly encircled me, in order for me to prostrate despite the crowd. One after the other, we formed with our bodies a solid triangular rampart so that our souls could meet. *The suffering of the forehead is good for our hearts.* Cosmic dance or spiritual trio, we could have inspired the most famous choreographs.

"...when their term comes, neither can they delay it nor can they advance it an hour (or a moment)."

Quran, Surah 7, Verse 34

The entire country was getting ready for Ramadhan. Our flight back to France was, sadly, set for the third day of this holy month. We had no choice.

On that night, at the hotel, the evening before the first day of fasting, the air we were breathing was lighter than usual. A gentle rain of peace and serenity was falling on us, falling from a musk cloud, hanging from the ceiling. I don't know if this is what human beings feel in the presence of Angels, but we never, really never, had been wrapped by such a well-being. We woke up to pray the night prayers, for a part of the night, then went back to sleep.

"Verily, those who say: "Our Lord is Allah (Alone)," and then they stand firm, on them the angels will descend (at the time of their death) (saying): "Fear not, nor grieve! But receive the glad tidings of Paradise which you have been promised! "We have been your friends in the life of this world and are (so) in the Hereafter. Therein you shall have (all) that your inner-selves desire, and therein you shall have (all) for which you ask."

Quran, Surah 41, verses 30 and 31.

Then, at the time of the prayer of *Fajr**, I found him, with a confident smile, his body relaxed with no sign of any contortion or pain, his right hand on top of his left hand, both on his chest, as if he was praying. He wasn't breathing anymore. I think he had met his Angels. He went back to God. His dream of dying in Medina had come true during his sleep, in the night of the first day of Ramadhan. He seemed to look ten years younger, his lips were heavenly pink, and his body was relaxed. A light was shining from him, and God guides towards His light whoever He wills. At that moment, because of the very special atmosphere, I couldn't really realise what was happening around me. I kissed him on his forehead and made wudhu. I wanted to keep him next to me just a bit more. Here, women don't accompany their dead to the grave.

A taste of eternity: this prayer of two units made me feel as if I was in another dimension. I had the feeling that I was floating. It was the first time that I felt my soul prostrating in my body. I can't remember what I told God during these moments. It's as if my ears had been covered by two big shells, I closed my eyes, my heart wept and I dived, I dived... within myself, 20,000 leagues under the earth.

While prostrating, I wanted to feel close to God, it was as if I was huddling together in my mother's womb. I was trying to immerse myself in the amniotic fluid which had protected me against exterior shocks, when I was an embryo.

I was looking for the matrix love, the status of the baby which endures and resorts to what it lived. But I had to give my *salam** to the Angels, I had to conclude this prayer by peace.

I phoned the reception of the hotel and they called the funeral services. They took care of everything. Everything seemed natural to them. Once the funeral bathing was done, a funeral prayer was performed for him in the mosque of the beloved Prophet, (peace and blessings be upon him). Then, a convoy of brothers gathered, applying the prophetic tradition, to accompany him to the grave. I wasn't allowed to join them.

Since then, I keep in mind the image of my husband as a pious and living man.

My flight back to France was planned two days after that, just enough time to deal with administrative work and gather our belongings. Our families, in France, were overwhelmed, but I hadn't realised yet what had happened. The flight back was horrible. I was filled with a feeling of void. The worse was meeting our families at my arrival. In their arms, I collapsed.

33 CM OR YEARS...

God created us as human beings and gifted us a potential, a human potential which we shouldn't despise, but rather use, within our limits and capacities, comprising our qualities and shortcomings, our needs and failures, our convictions, our questions, our doubts, our fears, our certainties and our oblivions... An abundance of ideas, thoughts, searches, projects and dreams... This is what my husband had always taught me. He used to tell me that the objectives of our transition on Earth, armed with all our potential, was to learn to reach deep within ourselves, to overcome the hardships of life and achieve our goals.

But which goal? To where, will you ask me? This is exactly the questions I asked myself when I was about to turn 33. It has been three weeks since I was back in France. Three weeks that we had been apart.

The straight line we draw to represent the curve of time is the one we are used to see from childhood in our history book, and it is still the one we use in the modern conception of duration. There is a beginning of dating of our arrival on Earth, then there is a timeline, a duration which shows the number of years that we will spend in this world. Our poor (or **rich**, it depends on what you want to write on this timeline) existence could **actually** be put on a short straight line. So, for me, if I had to draw it this way, my life would represent till today, a graduated rule of 33 cm... what about you?

We tend to draw, at the end of this timeline, an arrow pointing towards a goal, or a way back, it depends on the meaning we want to give to the days we spend here.

Philosophy diverges on this subject, but we can find with Plato a statement said by others, such as the philosopher Nietzsche: *"Time itself is a circle."* And this is what I can feel deep within myself. For me, it has nothing to do with reincarnation, nor with metempsychosis, nor with ignoring time in the choices, possibilities of change, human values that it contains, in what is new in it, unpredictable, individual, unique. I am not focused on the continuity of patterns which would continuously repeat themselves *ad vitam*.

But I invite you rather to a progression, on a loop road. To my mind, this return plays the role of an engine, it has to encourage us to harvest methods, knowledge, meetings here and there... which offer themselves to us, like provisions for the purpose of returning to our initial Essence, the one for which we have actually been created: the proximity of God. **The engine of life is its goal, the Return**... A return to myself for a return to God.

How could our representation of the world be changed, will you ask me, if we thought of time as a circle rather than as a line? Representing time as a circle opens up life perspectives which are completely different from the linear representation. In fact, the first reason for which I would give my attachment to this hypothesis is based on the verse of the Quran which reminds us **that we belong to God and to Him shall be our return.** So, the starting and the ending point are one and the same, like a loop.

Plato was once asked, at the end of his life, to give a last piece of advice about the meaning of life. His answer was: *"Learning how to live is learning how to die"*. In fact, living is learning how to return, to leave, to get rid of superficial things, to bear separations, to keep one's promises, engagements, to respect one's limits, to be satisfied with what we have...

What's more, thinking about time as a circle makes me think about the quranic verses which describe the succession of days and nights, during which we should pray and meditate. These hours and minutes which run and go by around the clock. The sun which sets, the moon which rises... The different cycles of nature... Our hormonal cycles as well. This circular vision of time also enables me to symbolically overcome trials, "the wheel is turning", as the saying goes. It reminds us of the notion of non-impunity, of return to the truth and judgement. It invites us to take chances, to protect oneself against risks in life. It also reminds us of the visit of the prophets, who also came to call us back to the inevitable or the long-awaited return.

THE WHEEL OF LIFE

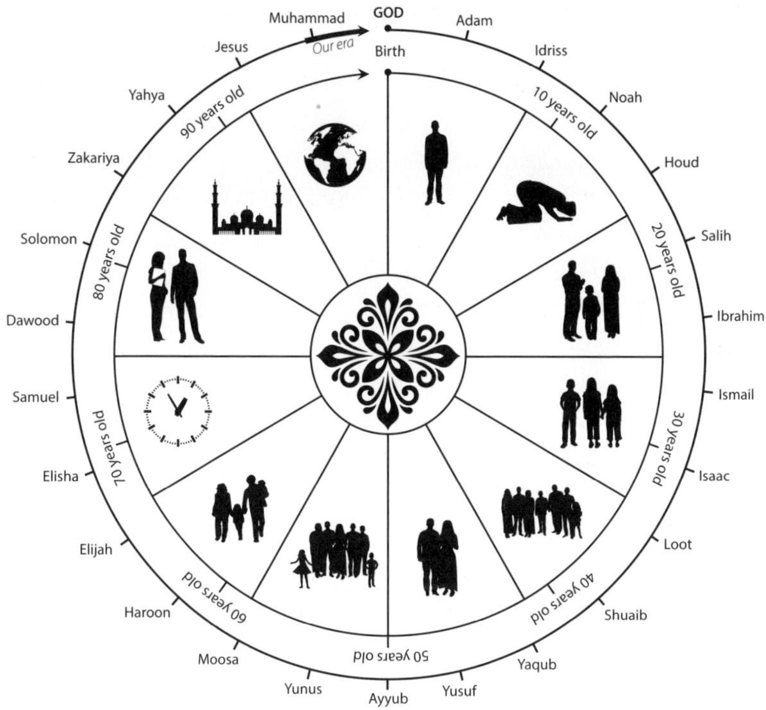

For a regulated, disciplined and just life, oriented towards a goal: loving God and being loved by Him.

God → *Adam*

The Prophets have been sent to remind us of this return to the Essential. We belong to the last era... every single detail of our life participates in the comprehensive plan.

Birth → 10 years old

Only God knows when we will return to Him!

OUR 12 ROLES ON EARTH

1: Human being
2: Muslim
3: Child of my parents
4: Member of my brotherhood and sisterhood
5: Member of my family
6: Spouse or future spouse
7: Member or future member of my in laws' family
8: Parent or future parent
9: Time manager in my life
10: Professional life, studies, hobbies 11: Member of my community, my brotherhood and sisterhood in God
12: Member of humanity

Circular time reminds me of the research made by Imam Al Ghazali, (may he rest in peace), who spoke about two types of revelation: *Al Wahyi Ad Dakhili* (inner revelation) and *Al Wahyi Al Khariji* (outer revelation). If we consider time as a loop, we would start by the inner revelation (linked to the reason and the fitra) in order to harvest, all along our life, during our earthly tour, *Al Wahyi Al Khariji* (external revelations - sciences of the holy scriptures revealed by God...) to nourish us and return to our state of *fitra*, even purer, richer in terms of experimentations and experiences, of the people you meet and with whom you share, of harvests and seeds...

Noorun Ala Noor, light upon light. From light, we have to return to light without extinguishing our light during our journey, but rather by shining. As the saying goes, there are two ways of shining, by being either the candle or the mirror... without forgetting that we are going back to the Source *An Noor* (one of the attributes of God).

The circular representation of time also reminds me of another geometric metaphor: the virtuous circle and the vicious circle and the round coherence of meaning that we want or can give to our lives. Our entire energy on earth will therefore be spent in trying to get into virtuous circles in order to come out of and to protect ourselves from vicious circles. Happiness is the circle, it is the virtuous path... I leave God, in fact, but to come back more loving. **Because for God, it is not the way that we went astray that matters, but the way we came back to Him...** Repenting means coming back and not forgetting that to err is human, and to persist in err is from the devil... And God is Merciful.

Muhammad Ibn Ad Duri said: "*The reasons for Satan's sadness are five:*
- *He refused to admit his sin,*
- *He didn't regret it,*
- *He didn't blame himself,*
- *He didn't show the willingness to repent,*
- *And he despaired about God's Mercy.*

Pride prevents from sincerely returning back to God. Sufyan At Thawri said:

"We can hope to be forgiven for any sin which was caused by temptation, but we cannot hope for it for sins caused by pride, because Satan's sin was caused by pride and Adam's sin by temptation".

The modern human being is proud and sick of time. He forgot the wisdom of the return and the meaning of his presence on Earth. God says, about this, in His Holy Book the Quran: *"They forget me and end up forgetting themselves"*... The great despair for these men and women of these modern times is the feeling that their lives don't lead to **anything**. But it isn't the case! The solution is to remember that we are returning back to The Almighty... and not to nothing.

We return to The Almighty, The All-knowing, The Self-Sufficient, the Omnipotent, The All-Merciful, and in our lives, everything is a **reminder**. In fact, God put prophets, individuals, books in our path as well as in our hearts, feelings, sensations, and in our souls, states and remorse. All of these are signs, signs we should pay attention to. Because if we aren't paying attention to everything we can listen to, harvest and sow on **Earth**, it is as if someone told us to do a world trip, back and forth from Paris, without any stop... What's the point?

And this is what thousands of our brothers and sisters, who haven't found the meaning they want to give to their lives yet, feel. Martin Luther King said this powerful statement: *"If you haven't* ***found*** *anything worth dying for, then you aren't meant to live".* I have always been filled with a biological idealism, truly willing to treat my neighbour as if he/she was already the person he/she should be. I had always wanted to help him/her become the person he/she is capable of becoming.

Life is always a work in progress; but one shouldn't forget to live the present, and to act for our future. What is the work in progress? It is the state in which we will be at the time of our return... Richer? At least in terms of faith, I hope.

At the end of their lives, rare are the people who regret not having earned enough money. Most of them regret not having visited some places, their family members who they abandoned, the risks they didn't take, the verses they haven't learned, the opportunities they missed, the feelings they didn't express... It is only forgetting themselves, forgetting their purpose on Earth, the accumulation of sins, which lead the human beings away from their inner being.

Carl Jung said in his book *Modern Man in Search of a Soul*: *"In these last thirty years, people from all over the world came to ask me for advice and I cured hundreds of sick people, most of them were in the middle of their lives, which means that they were above 35 years old, and none but all of them were looking for religious help to aspire to life. Therefore, I can say: each one of them had fallen sick because they didn't have what religion offers to a believer and none of them will ever be healed, until their* ***true faith*** *comes back."*

The needs for self-actualization and spirituality are inscribed within human nature. Like an archaeologist on the field, I think that, under these waste lands, under this skeleton, there are hidden treasures... I think that the biggest inhibitor of human potential is fear. It is fear, which prevents human beings to trust their compass, their hearts. *"Oh human, in fact, you are limited and you are a mere mortal, but if you want to be the strongest and the wisest of men, then put your trust in God and be a good person."*

The human being needs models of excellence that he can observe and imitate, like the prophets and the pious men.

Excellence is pushed to a veritable paroxysm to target and tend towards this ideal. We might be different, but we all have potentials, as if we all were "HB" (human beings) branded computers, but what will change are the processors that we will install in ourselves, the software that we will download and develop, and the anti-viruses that we will use, that's what will make the difference. We will also progressively have to format some of our preconceptions.

The world surrounding us displeases me, but I think that we firstly have to do a major cleansing, to polish our hearts, to change our concepts, to start to prepare for change, to start to think: "How can I be useful in order to make this global change happen?" The world in which we live is just the reflection of the state of mind in which we are as an individual, and it is our role to make our consciences unite for and around the universal Good. It is our role to rediscover our principles, to make the link with our convictions and to protect our spiritual ecology...

"That is so because Allah will never change a grace which He has bestowed on a people until they change what is in their own selves. And verily, Allah is All-Hearer, All-Knower."

(Quran, Surah 8, verse 53)

I am not a stargazer, I am an actress... Yes, actress of my destiny. I run my own marathon, no one else's. A famous man was once asked, on his death bed: "What would you do if you could live your life again?" He thought and replied with a deep sigh: "I would like to be the person I could have been, but who I never was". I write these lines today in my diary, so that this never happens to me... so that I live in the body, with the heart, and the soul of the person that I can and want to be, that is to say me.

THE LETTER

I had a very dark look on life, a single haunting thought was resonating in my head: "What good would it do?" I had the feeling, that nothing had meaning anymore, that nothing was worth it, I had the feeling that I was alive only when I was prostrating.

On that morning, I mustered the courage and, after having cleaned and sorted the house a bit, I went out for a walk. I was holding firmly my MP3 player. I was listening to Quran, again and again... *"Verily, in the remembrance of Allâh do hearts find rest"* *(Surah 13, verse 28).*

A quick look at the mailbox suddenly paralysed me. I thought that I had recognised my husband's writing. On a pile of ads, there was a letter which, indeed, seemed different. A thick envelope, my first name, my surname, my address were written by the hand of my husband, a month after his death. My whole body started shivering, I came back in to open it in a safe place. Drops of sweat were dropping from my forehead, my hands were sweaty. My heart was beating so fast, that I only managed to put the key inside the lock after many attempts. Once the door was closed behind me, all my body collapsed, I couldn't walk any further. I delicately opened the letter, as if I was handling something fragile, which could fall down and break.

Ten pages, linked by a clip, written by my husband's very hand, how can this be possible?

I might be mistaken, maybe it's from someone else? His handwriting? I could have recognised it out of hundred others. He was left-handed and used to write very small. And this quote, at the back of this letter, would exactly be his kind of saying. ***"There are no mistakes in life, there are only lessons.*** *There is no negative experience, there are only opportunities to grow, to learn and to move along the way of self-mastery, along the way of humility before Allah. Strength comes from the battle. Even pain can be a teacher."*

I am afraid, what is this letter about? I am afraid but I am eager to understand. Here is what I received this Monday morning at 11.

All praise is due to Allah, peace and blessings be upon the Prophet, his family and his companions.

Dear and loving wife,
If you receive this letter, it means that I'm no longer part of this world. If you receive this letter, it means that my soul has given its shell back to the Earth. She went back to God, satisfied and accepting His decree.

During these years that we spent together, we have been a garment for each other. Don't shiver while reading this letter, it will also be a garment to you. Even if I am physically not there anymore, I will morally and spiritually guide you. Each time you would want to hug me, read my letter, my words will warm your heart.

I will help you bear this momentary separation with divine help. You just need to apply my advice and recommendations, and you will never be sad again neither on Earth, nor in the Hereafter. In order to do so, I have laid some foundations which will prevent you from falling or will help you bounce back all along your journey in this world.

Have you realised, how, even after his death, your husband is there, behind you... Are you smiling?... Come on, wipe your tears and remember, among the books which we had read together, what Victor Hugo had said: "The biggest happiness in life is to be convinced that we are loved." I love you, my soul loves you, my soul is still alive, never forget this. And also receive this news, that God loves you. Through this separation, He wants to teach you detachment and approval, important steps on the path of every Muslim. He loves you and wants you to be strong. Of course, you will have moments of weakness, but never despair, never despair of God's help and mercy.

He tells you: "I am that which my servant thinks of Me". Think that God will help you and He will help you. Only think good about Him. It's not because you've been tested that you should forget all the blessings that God showered you with. God says: "and if you count the Blessings of Allah, never will you be able to count them." (Surah 14, verse 34) Don't forget to thank God for your faith. Don't ruminate, don't rehash, don't focus on the past, this attitude spreads anxiety and melancholy. "Be not sad (or afraid), surely Allah is with us." (Surah 9, verse 40) Your sadness won't bring you back to yourself, and I don't want you to be sad. You will live the time which has been decreed for you, as I lived mine and we will meet again. Yesterday doesn't belong to you anymore, tomorrow doesn't belong to you yet. Enjoy today, don't waste your time, don't ground the flour a second time. Don't hold on to your past, don't dramatize the future, nothing depends on you, you have been created only to do your best, no more and no less. For now, live day by day, saying to yourself that you will feel better than yesterday. Apply the verse of God which says: "So hold that which I have given you and be of the grateful." (Surah 7, verse 144)

You're not the only one to experience separation, use this test to help the people who, like you, have been tested. Don't bury yourself alive, and especially, don't isolate yourself. Inoccupation, isolation and the absence of goals and objectives are torture for your soul, don't grieve it and don't be unjust and harsh with it. What struck you could have never missed you and what will miss you could have never struck you.

God says: "And certainly, We shall test you with something of fear, hunger, loss of wealth, lives and fruits, but give glad tidings to As-Sâbirun (the patient)" (Surah 2, verse 155). "See they not that they are put in trial once or twice every year (with different kinds of calamities, disease, famine)?" (Surah 9, verse 126)

Dear spouse, I loved, I love and I will always love your personality, don't change, don't become harsh, embittered. Keep smiling to the orphans and the poor. Don't refuse happiness and the opportunities that will come to you, they come from God.

Keep your joy of living while nourishing your joy of the return. The one which loves meeting Allah loves meeting him, so prepare yourself to it. Teach your soul to submit to Destiny and fate. "Wheresoever you may be, death will overtake you even if you are in fortresses built up strong and high!" (Surah 4, verse 78) Sincere love has neither borders nor a limited time, invocations and prayers reach me. Wake up and pray at night, beg God to help you bear with peace and serenity. He is The One Who responds to the calls of the one who is cornered by his sorrows when he implores Him. When a problem preoccupied the Prophet, peace and blessings be upon him, he used to say: "O Bilal! Give us comfort and call for the Salaat". Plan breaks within your program during which you will write your worries down, in front of each one, think of possible solutions. Once this handbook of worries closed, forbid yourself to think about it until your next break. It's up to you to define the frequency of breaks. But not more than once a day.

The best worship for you will be to wait for the liberation, prostrated in front of His door at night, and active during the day.

God tells you: "Believe and act upon it." Never fall into boredom and diversify your acts. A wonderful life, rich in good deeds and knowledge, isn't something you get through memories or while dreaming or drowsing, but through resolutions, determination and causes which you constantly renew.

As I know you, I guess you stopped eating properly. Remember that your body has a right upon you, it is your soul's horse. The more you will take care of it, the further it will take you. I will help you have better health practices. I prepared some surprises for you. Take the meaning of life as it is. The life in this world is mixed, you will find good things as well as upsetting things. "Or think you that you will enter Paradise without such (trials) as came to those who passed away before you? They were afflicted with severe poverty and ailments and were so shaken that even the Messenger and those who believed along with him said, "When (will come) the Help of Allah?"" (Surah 2, verse 214). Work on your heart, prepare it for the Hereafter. Make it long for eternity, peace and justice. Make it want to meet the Messengers. Make it love the proximity of Angels. Know that pleasure comes from the outside and happiness comes from within.

"Blessed is He in Whose Hand is the dominion, and He is Able to do all things. Who has created death and life, that He may test you which of you is best in deed. And He is the All-Mighty, the Oft-Forgiving..." (Surah 67, verses 1 and 2). Read this Surah every evening, it will protect you in your grave.

Even though you know that everything is temporary, don't prohibit yourself from appreciating the creation and bliss of Allah, and don't feel guilty for things for which you're not responsible. "Our Lord! You have not created (all) this without purpose." (Surah 3, verse 191)

You will have to find your balance. For the moment, you're focused on fear and loss of confidence in life, ask God for hope and success in this life and in the next.

"And it may be that you dislike a thing which is good for you and that you like a thing which is bad for you. Allah knows but you do not know." (Surah 2, verse 216)

Ibn al Wazeer said in his book Al Awassim min al Qawasim (lightning rods and disasters): "Hope is in Allah's Grace, The Glorious, The Majestic, to give to His servant the hope, to help him in his obedience and to give him energy in order for him to accomplish the voluntary deeds and to devote himself to blessings."

Your mandatory prayers aren't sufficient, help yourself with voluntary prayers. They are additional guarantees for you. Fast and pray twelve units of prayer in the day and eleven in the night. These spiritual remedies have saved many depressed hearts. "If you give thanks (by accepting Faith and worshipping none but Allah), I will give you more (of My Blessings)" (Surah 14, verse 7).

Don't be disappointed by your relatives. Don't get angry, they are also scared of what you are experiencing. Have a compassionate look towards them. "And say to My slaves (i.e. the true believers of Islamic Monotheism) that they should (only) say those words that are the best. (Because) Shaitan (Satan) verily, sows state of conflict and disagreements among them." (Surah 17, verse 53). They are only humans who are ungrateful and neglectful towards their own Lord. The Prophet Moses, peace and blessings be upon him, asked God to silence those who were criticising him, and God told him: "O Mussa! I didn't even do it for Myself, I create them, I maintain them, and they insult Me and offend Me."

Use their negative points to love the Hereafter, don't clutter up your mind and be a beneficial person. This hardship should make you forgiving. Be demanding only towards yourself, let the others be accountable to their Lord. Perhaps, God considered that they aren't ready to understand certain things. Because each thing happens at its given time. May God enable you to become a blessing for the inhabitants of the Earth, as much as you were for me.

Your heart doesn't want to read, it doesn't want to do anything, force it. The books on our bookshelf are within reach, day and night, don't deprive yourself from these loyal companions. Sleep only when it's time to sleep, don't think you will forget the meaning of life by sleeping/in your sleep. Be most of the time in a state of ablution. Say the invocations of the morning and the evening, they will be a blessing for you. Ask God to introduce you to the knowledge which will be useful to you for this life and the Hereafter. "Allah will grant after hardship, ease." (Surah 65, verse 7)

Don't stop that to which you had committed yourself. After I've left, the Earth kept turning, didn't it? Imagine you are on stairs and that the steps below are crumbling down, what is the only thing you can do? Climb my sweetheart, go up the ladder, stop only to catch your breath. Don't be scared to believe in your projects, if they are on the path of divine satisfaction, use your mind and construct, build stone by stone and don't break the ties of kinship.

You will have to swim against the stream for a while. Ask God to protect you from lack of willpower and laziness. Merit belongs to the one who begins, even though the next one does better. Your whole being doesn't want to hear what I am saying because it knows I am right. You know that what I am telling you is right, but you are weary. Yet, I advise you precisely fast-acting sugar to fight weariness. Do your best and God will help you. Diamonds are made under very high pressure. Also think about delegating, dare to ask, don't become arrogant, you need your fellows, ask those who are close to God. It isn't the event that you are experiencing which is dramatic, it's what you're going to make out of it which might be.

Don't use my departure as a pretext to your sadness. Your timer hasn't stopped yet, so you shouldn't stop either. Live, live in perpetual remembrance, and you will be happy. Each day is a new day. Let it flow, stagnant water is bad, it infects and will affect you. The most modest action is worth more than the noblest intention.

When Ibn Taymiyyah had a difficult problem to solve, he would beg God for forgiveness a thousand times, and he would find the solution. Follow our predecessors and pray for them.

God said: "Whoever works righteousness, whether male or female, while he (or she) is a true believer verily, to him We will give a good life" (Surah 16, verse 97). "O man! Verily, you are returning towards your Lord with your deeds and actions (good or bad), a sure returning, and you will meet" (Surah 84, verse 6). "Verily, those who believe and work deeds of righteousness, the Most Gracious will bestow love for them" (Surah 19, 96). You are brave, even though you doubt it, because God doesn't make us bear that which we can not bear. Don't abandon your past ambitions, persevere with dignity and respect.

If you need to hear me speaking to you, read me again. If you want to hear God speaking to you, read His revealed words in the Quran. If you want to speak to Him, pray. If you want to talk to me, start by greeting the Prophet, peace and blessings be upon him, the Angels, all the Prophets, those which followed them, and pray for your family and invoke God in my favour.

Perhaps God will allow me to come in your dreams to advise you. The closest you will be to God, the closest you will be to me. Because your soul will be sensible to the realm of the Hereafter. True success in your life will result from an inner work. A tedious work on the path of knowledge and self-fulfilment. Focus on the things which matter the most in your life, don't pressure yourself into doing too many things and be fair towards yourself and others, God will be pleased with you.

Read this letter again and again, as much as you need it. Apply its advice. This first letter is only the start of a great complicity between us...

Fraternally, your husband
I love you in God and I trust you.

P.S.: Back to your essentially heavenly being... Live every day of your life as if you were climbing up a mountain. Every day, look towards the summit to remind yourself of your goal. Establish observation points to replenish your stock and contemplate the Majesty of Allah through His creation and His creatures. Climb slowly and pay attention, with a regular and sure pace, avoid clefts and false shortcuts, but rather walk on the footsteps of the Prophets, the truthful, the pious, the martyrs and the righteous. Take time to humbly appreciate every single moment and the view that Allah will give you at the arrival will be the climax which you deserve after your journey in this life. The Prophet, peace and blessings be upon him, said one day to Abu Dharr Al Ghiffari: "Oh Abu Dharr! Restore your ship, for the sea is deep. Take your provisions perfectly, for the journey is long. Lighten your load, for the ascent is steep. Be sincere in your acts, for the Watchful One sees everything."

I read these pages a million times at least with my heart, my eyes, and all my understanding. My husband was a farsighted man. But I would have never imagined such a scenario. Masha Allah*! He even thought about supporting me in case he would have been the first to leave. Maybe God had informed him, maybe not. I will find out only in the Hereafter.

This letter had the effect of a cold shower. Every advice had the effect of an electroshock. As a precaution, I had the reflex of copying it. I directly hid the original letter.

I prepared herbal tea and with a highlighter, I dissected word by word the richness and profound statements of this letter. I looked for the immediate meaning, and the hidden meaning. I tried to put these enlightening pieces of advice into context. I also wrote in my notebook those which I could already start applying and **in the order** in which I could apply them. I planned them somehow. This firstly helped me fix myself. I sorted out the pieces of advice for which I would need help, support and companionship. I ended up knowing the letter by heart.

Seeing myself act this way with the letter reminded me of the warning of a sister who said, during a preach: "If your true love writes you a letter, how will you react? You will certainly be very careful with it, you will read it again and again, hoping to find something new each time you read it, which will make you love him even more. And what if he tells you it's his last letter? You will pay even more attention to it." And the sister raised our awareness about the fact that God revealed to us a last letter: the Quran, but sadly, we often forget it. We let dust cover it, shamelessly. I have experienced what the sister described myself. She is right, our True Love is God, we shouldn't hit the wrong target. "O you who believe! Let not your properties or your children divert you from the remembrance of Allah." (Surah 63, verse 9)

BACK TO YOUR ESSENTIAL HEAVENLY BEING

I invite every single reader to do like me. Pretend this letter was written to you. Close your eyes, and let the wisdom of its words fill you. It contains universal and timeless advice. Read it and read it over and over again and you will see that each time, it will touch a different part of your being. Because in the meantime, other hardships or questions will have come to you. You are constantly in progress in the school of growth which is life. Underline that which rings a bell to you today, that which seems to affect you. Write down what is missing for you to make it come true. Say what touched you and how?

Do this exercise on paper, in order to grasp the meaning of your existence and to accept that the things which are happening to you, good or needing courage, encapsulate all a divine and beneficial lesson. It is vital for you to assimilate it, at this very particular stage of your life. The purpose is to find the right balance between letting go and controlling. Letting go your entire life without using your practical sense and without elaborating a plan for your life isn't what God is expecting from you. Same thing with devoting yourself to controlling, thinking that we will be able to manage and program everything, this isn't what God is expecting from you either. The purpose is to go back and forth between I program, I plan, I organise, I take actions and I let go. The result belongs to God once I have done humanely the most I can.

• Underline with a pencil the passages that touched you in this chapter and copy them in your notebook, precising what touched you.

• Inspiring yourself from the chapter 33 cm or years, draw in your notebook a timeline of your life, writing down the decisive dates and periods that built the person you are today.

• For those who want it, and feel they have the strength to do it, write a letter with advice for your relatives, using the letter of the husband as an inspiration.
• Ask yourself the following question: "Why did God want me to read this book?" Everything you will read in it is meant for you, no doubt about it!

Bonus Point...
Learn by heart the verses of the Quran in the text, they have special virtues and hearts find rest with them...

A FORTY-SIXTH PART OF PROPHECY

According to Abu Hurayra, may God be pleased with him, the Prophet, peace and blessings be upon him, said: "People whose hearts are like the hearts of birds will enter paradise." *(Muslim)* It is said that it means they rely on Allah like birds do. It is also said that their hearts are sensible like the one of birds. I would have loved to fly like these birds, accompany my husband's soul and know that he is safe, but my mission on Earth has been extended... Until when? Only God knows. For now, I need to trust and keep **Existing**, use my wings to Resist and Understand, Read and Draw, Listen and Write, Transmit and Sow, in order to better **recover myself**.

I woke up at the time of Fajr with a strange feeling in my mouth. My vocal cords were knotted and my tongue was pasty. I drink a glass of water, take ablutions, but nothing changes. I suddenly recall the dream I had that night. I dreamt that someone was reciting the following verse to me: "Your sign is that you shall not speak to mankind for three days except with signals. And remember your Lord much, and glorify (Him) in the afternoon and in the morning". *(Quran, Surah 3, verse 41)*

Sitting on the edge of my bed, no sound could come out of my mouth. Holding my head in my hands, I was trying to shout, to scream, but to no avail! Nothing comes out! But perhaps it is useless to fight against fate...

Have I become speechless?! If I think about the verse revealed, it should last three days... or maybe more? May God grant us patience, but I want to recover my voice now. I'm panicking... I'm going crazy, what should I do? Should I go to the emergency services? Should I go to a speech pathologist? Is it linked to the emotional shock? I take my Quran and read the entire Surah from which the verse is extracted... I try to understand, shaking, what's happening within me. The beginning of the verse is: ""O my Lord! Make a sign for me." Said Zachary".

Of course! That's it! I have asked God for a sign this night before going to sleep. But why taking my voice away from me? Am I not alone enough since my husband left me? Have I not been tested enough? What is the fact of not being able to speak supposed to create within me? Should I dig deeper? The Prophet, peace and blessings be upon him, said: *"Dreams are of three types: one good dream which is a sort of good tidings from Allah; the evil dream which causes pain is from the satan; and the third one is a suggestion of one's own mind".* *(Bukhari and Muslim).*

Abu Hurayra, may God be pleased with him, said: "I heard the Prophet, peace and blessings be upon him, say: "From the prophecy are left the announcers of glad tidings." We said: "And who are the announcers of glad tidings?" He said: "Authentic dreams."" *(Bukhari)*. Narrated by Abu Hurayra again, the Prophet, peace and blessings upon him, said: "When the time draws near (when the Resurrection is near) a believer's dream can hardly be false. And the truest vision will be of one who is himself the most truthful in speech, for the vision of a Muslim is the forty-fifth part of Prophecy." *(Bukhari)*

"Say: "Travel in the land"

(Quran, Surah 6, verse 11)

In order to try to understand, I read a book of oneiromancy *Interpretation of dreams* by Ibn Sirin (7th century). I read that, according to the author, the *Surah Imran's family* announces many travels... Perhaps I will travel someday... Who knows?

However, I understand thanks to this new trial, that I firstly need to learn how to travel within myself to discover new lands and new corners. Draw, deepen, excavate my being, while glorifying and imploring my God! I need to dig and find refuge. Find refuge within myself, in my cave, take a spiritual retreat, a silent trip... this voiceless experience surely means that?!

I have to search like a field archaeologist. The word "archaeologist" comes from ancient Greek ἀρχαιολογία and is formed thanks to the roots ἀρχαῖος =

ancient and λόγος = word/ speech/ oration. Has God taken my voice away so that I consider from now on a preventive search in my soul? The purpose of archaeology is to study and reconstitute the history of humanity, thanks to all the material traces which remain and which sometimes need to be revealed. **Should I reveal some things thanks to the traces and remnants of my personal story?**

Despite my fear, I am sure that this experience coming from God will reveal within me a lot of blessings. It's surely there, in this depth, in the corners of my spirit, in this zone which remains unknown to me, in this cave where my most personal choices are elaborated, that my thought arise, that it grows and becomes stronger, that it finds justifications and stimulations. These upsides and undersides will be as many supports and backings for my future life. I shouldn't worry then. I just need to learn how to read the hieroglyph written on the walls of my heart. Speaking about my heart, my husband had offered me a mug once, on which my name was written in hieroglyph:

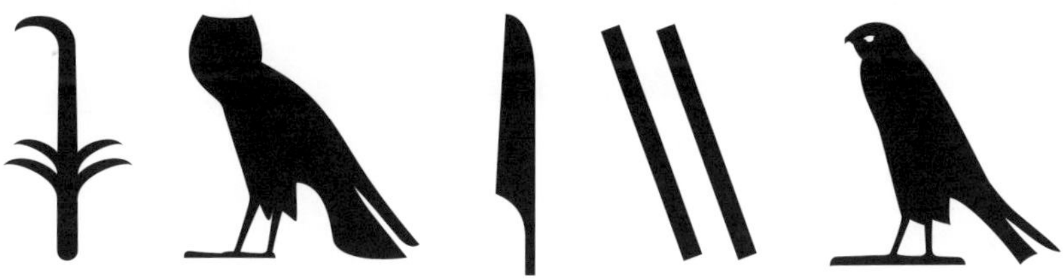

My name was the one of a pious and very brave woman... May God give us the piety and courage to bear fate as well as she did during her life.

Isolate yourself in a peaceful place, sit down or lie down for fifteen minutes and nurture the art of silence. Don't speak to anyone. Don't write. Don't read. Think as little as possible. Disengage intellectually. Imagine that your spirit is a lake, and try to make it as flat as a mirror. (...) Listen to the "voice of silence", deep breath of beauty, of harmony...

Norman Vincent Peale

I know that all the disharmonies, all the imbalances and the existential shocks within me are closely linked to the perception that I have of my own person, especially after my husband's death. By the way, since then even my sight became blurred. I have a blurred vision... I don't have self-confidence anymore. I have the feeling that I've been forced to enter a labyrinth without being able to come out of it. God took my voice away today, but until when? I have no idea. I just know that I can't ask for my way... Shouldn't I find my way within me? Isn't it deep within ourselves that we can find the answers? Isn't it at the source that we will find energy?

The problem is that when I find myself alone with myself, alone in my "inner library", all the events, all the actions experienced, all the past deeds, all my missed acts, all the emotions or feelings that I experienced are there, I can see them on these shelves.

Everything is stored in my head. My subconscious, in its quest for information, has even stored for each memorised event the emotional load which goes with it. The problem is also that these projections start without my consent. How to make it stop?

Are these scenes lessons? Will they stop once I have learned the fundamentals and acquired the basics? This underground shooting of my past, where nothing goes forgotten, nothing goes lost, down to the most indescribable feelings, is it meant to contribute to making me become what I can be?

"Who isn't master over his thoughts, can become their slave" as the saying goes. I don't want to be slave to my thoughts, nor to my past. When I let my thoughts develop crossing my conscience, I have this feeling of blockage, it's as if my head was going to burst. My spirit is full of drives and ideas, of images and representation, each one more pessimistic and morbid than the others. This silence prescribed by God is like a prescription from the doctor, a treatment which encourages me to take a closer look at these "wandering" thoughts. I notice that my thoughts which enjoyed until then total freedom, because of my disinterest, gather together, become amalgamated and end up creating knots,

knots of thoughts. These knots are obstacles which prevent the free flow of "mother thoughts", of my "true thoughts", of my "right thoughts", those which get things moving, those which make me the actor of my destiny.

They harm the positive flow of *Haqqi Tawakkul*, within me, of this true "I sincerely rely on God".

FIRST CRY...

Realising, says Bernard Baudouin, the role of our thoughts, firstly consists in questioning the exact nature of everything that comes through and occupies our mind all day long. Because our thoughts shape our vision of life. We have to learn how to master the fundamentals of our own dynamics. Meditation, he says, is an adventure, a trip within the heart of man, which tends to bring him back to his roots in order to make him understand who he truly is. This silence is an invitation to meditation.

It is about opening yourself to yourself, revealing your essential being, deeply liberating yourself. In spite of all the outside pressures of the modern world, meditating is about reconnecting with our inner universe, where all our potentials are found, our most individual and authentic richness, where our energy is regenerated, where our hopes come to life and our ability to make them come true.

Before going back to God, my husband had started to read a lot. He used to tell me: "Know that the ability to think is, without any doubt, the biggest blessing that God has given to mankind after the physical ability to live". It is up to us to take advantage of it, to make a major asset out of it, and above all, not to let anyone rob this invaluable richness. He used to compare the mind to a fertile field. He used to say that if we nourish it, if we cultivate it like the owner of a garden does, it would produce even more flowers than what we expected.

But if you let noxious weeds grow, or someone assume ownership over your thoughts, your peace of mind (*Sakina*) and deep inner harmony will always slip out of your hands. He said to me: "Tell me, if you had a splendid garden, which was rich and could give fruits in abundance, would you let anyone or anything shed toxic material on it?"

I had answered: "Of course not!" Actually, most of the gardeners guard their gardens like loyal sentinels and make sure that nothing contaminates them. And yet, look at all the toxic material that we shed on our minds. He told me: "In order to live in serenity and spirituality, and in a rich and blossoming way, you have to guard the door of your garden and let only the best information come in and circulate, those which educate you, those which protect you, those which are true, soft, right, wise and non-violent." **"And remember your Lord much, and glorify Him in the afternoon and in the morning."** *(Quran, Surah 3, verse 41)*

Some wise men used to forbid themselves from any negative thought. Because for them they had to educate their mind to *Husnu Dhan*. "To have a good opinion of God and the people." Each time a negative thought or a **doubt** would cross their minds, they regarded it as a noxious weed and would take it out of their hearts by fasting.

"When you were born, you cried while the world was rejoicing. Live so that when you die, the world will cry but you will be the one rejoicing."

Wisdom

This is what my husband trained for the rest of his life. He wanted to be vigilant and responsible. His goal was the "vigilant thought". By the way, it's the title of a book by Ibn Al Jawzi (1120-1201) that we read together. I found this book on our bookshelf. In his letter, didn't my husband write: ***"Your heart doesn't want to read, it doesn't want to do anything, force it to. The books on our bookshelf are at reach day and night, don't forbid yourself from these loyal companions..."***, did he? And God knows that today, more than yesterday, I really need companions to enlighten me.

This book starts by the following sentences: *"Praises be to God! Praises which satisfy Him. May Allah bless the noblest that He chose, those who live with Him and are His allies! May He grant them a status which has no end.* ***O how my thoughts are floating*** *when they turn the pages of the great book of things which opens in front of them,* ***o how fast then, they turn away and disappear****, it seemed essential to me* ***to prevent them from escaping towards oblivion.*** *"Write down knowledge" said the Prophet, peace and blessings be upon him. So many ideas came to my mind which I couldn't write down and which escaped, leaving me full of regrets! When I open my reflecting eyes in front of the divine mystery, the wonders which it contains* *reveal themselves numerously to my sight and explications which I can't silence, pile up in front of me like sand on a dune.*

Therefore, this book is meant to be a net to catch escaping ideas..."

As a result, he wrote a book of 306 pages gathering his thoughts, his butterflies of the day. Such a simple but fertile idea, which allowed him to leave positive traces of his journey on Earth. And people keep reading again and again this author more than 800 years after his death (may he rest in peace). **If I were to cast a net like Sheikh Ibn Al Jawzi did for his thoughts, what would I like to find in it? What would I like to catch in it? Which positive traces of my journey will I be able to leave on Earth? Why have I been created? What are my missions? How can I be useful?** So many questions which are essential to me, without which I can't imagine the future... I have to resolve not to be worried by the only fact of having to earn a living alone now. And this is how the true meaning of earning a Living with a capital "L". **What meaning do we give to our work? To our salary? To our studies? To our efforts?** So many essential questions to me...

For the first time my heart cries silently, it's as if something took my breath away... We cry at the time of our birth. This cry is the expression of our first breath. But this cry should also remind us of how birth represents a brutal and enormous change in order to adapt to a new world.

A brutal and enormous change?! I actually just experienced one. What about you? Since he left, I have to adapt to a new world. And God invites me to come to life again silently, to get to know myself better, to be reborn to knowing myself better soundlessly. But why? I'm sure that it is in order to revive my life... Victor Frankl said something important: *"Success, as much as happiness, can't be pursued. It must manifest. And it only manifests as a secondary effect* ***of devotion to a cause greater than oneself..."*** But for that, I must accept that every hardship in my life is an occasion given to me by God to come back to life taller, bigger, riper, more mature and purer.

Religion, if it happens to make the people whose spirits are elevated speechless, it makes those who have nothing to say even more talkative.

Roger Lemellin

I can remember that this exciting subject was the centre of our discussions during several weeks... I learned with him with surprise that during one day around sixty thousand thoughts run through the mind of an ordinary person. And that 95% of these 60 000 daily thoughts are the same as the day before. We aren't able to master the climate, because it isn't our function. But we have so many other abilities which we usually ignore. In fact, we have a God-given power and a mission to control **our attitude** and **our thoughts** concerning the events which happen in our lives. We all have the necessary potential given by God to choose what we want to think about an event in our lives. This capacity is part of what makes us human. Sheikh Aid Al Qarni narrates the story of two poets who were put into jail during the revolution. They were staring through the window of their cell: the first one was staring at the stars and smiled, while the other one, he was staring at the mud in a nearby street and cried. *"This world is a prison for the believer"*... as the Prophet, peace and blessings be upon him, said.

It is up to us to choose what we want to look at from the windows of our lives. The mud or the stars?

Whatever happens in our lives, we are the only ones, who have the ability of choosing how we will react. Having the habit of looking for positive elements in every circumstance allows us to give bigger dimensions to life. And all of this happens when we use our garden (our spirit) more efficiently. Because our inner world will influence our outside world. This willingness to **always** stay positive, will, as a result, end up bringing positivity to our everyday life. By controlling what we think and the way we react to events, we start being actors of our destiny. This art of thinking encourages us to educate our hearts to the fact that there are only opportunities to progress on the way of **self-control**.

In order to have a fertile garden, spirit, we have to protect it, remove any toxicity from it and maintain it with positive thoughts and *Dhikr**. And in order to liberate the potential of our mind, we have to develop our imagination, our intentions and our dreams. A previous teacher told me when I was a child: "When we stop dreaming, we die"... All of this, I learned it with him...

God endowed us with a factory, our mind, our intentions, from there come our concepts, our ideas, our processes, our prototypes... and then, and only if God wills, the fruits of our work will come into reality and materialise. Yet, we can't materialise the inexistent in our intentions.

What are my intentions this year? What about you? When we learn how to master our thoughts and that we clearly imagine them, all that which we want to do in our earthly life, the forces and energy which were sleeping within us suddenly wake up. We then begin liberating our True potential, the one of our intention of wanting to make these objectives come true for God's sake. **But what about me, today, have I forgotten about my dreams? Or have I just resigned myself to a usual boring life, like all the adults are supposed to do nowadays?**

During the weeks when we were discussing with my husband, I recall an exercise which he told me to do about my dreams. I actually kept it in a box under my bed. This exercise was called **"The 101 things I dream of doing before I die".** I really want to read again what I wrote then. I can remember having thought: "101 things, but that's not enough", but once in front of the blank page, I realised that the exercise was much harder than it seemed. I actually didn't even finish this list. Isn't this morning the perfect time to finish it?

By writing down my real dreams and true objectives on a sheet of paper, I raise a kind of red flag in front of my unconscious, in order to tell it that this perfect and complete thought is way more important than the 59,999 others which swirl in my head. If I focus my mind to fulfil my objectives, I will pay more attention to all the opportunities to make them come true... In order to explain this to me, my husband had taken the example of a purple dress. He told me: "If you buy a purple dress, as I know you, you will want to match the colours with the rest of your outfit. So your mind will be focused in front of the shops windows looking for all the purple accessories. It is the same with your objectives, once they are written down, all your unconscious will be on alert each time you will pass by a tool which would help you to make it come true."

One of the prices of success, tough and expensive to pay in the Hereafter is the price of the responsibility of each of our thoughts, because what they induce has heavy consequences in our lives... What scholars of all time recommend is to take 10 minutes every morning and 10 minutes every evening to dedicate to our goals and to the way we live our life daily. As Robin Sharma says: *"Saying that you don't have time to improve your thoughts and your life is like saying you don't have time to stop for gas because you're too busy driving."* But one day, reality will catch up and you will be out of gas.

"The purpose of life is to live a life full of purpose."

Martin Luther King

I stand up and go towards the cupboard. I need to look at myself in the mirror, but what I see scares me... it isn't me?! I have dark circles under the eyes, my hair became dull, I lost too much weight, I am insipid, colourless, odourless, transparent, I am out of gas and broken down. I stopped taking myself into consideration, and respecting myself since he left. This silence forces me to scan my soul. How can it want to feel better in such a body? One of the keys of self-discipline, responsibility and spiritual edification consists in taking care of your inner being, but I forgot myself... I forgot who I am and who I want to be.

It is Carl Jung who said: *"Your vision becomes clear only once you can look into your heart. The one who looks outside dreams; the one who looks inside awakes."* I lost my voice to recover my sight. When God **pushes us away from our usual comfort zone**, it is to educate us to sustainable self-control and to maximise our True Potential. Thus, we must quietly contemplate where we are coming from and where we are heading to.

I understand with every passing hour of this endless morning where I didn't stop talking to you, that introspection is really a divine tool that we should use daily, in order to consider with greater objectivity and preliminary reflection all of our decisions, all of our choices, all our actions at the present time.

It is 9:30 am, I suddenly feel sick, I must deal with some administrative documents. It's been ages since I have last taken public transportation and I must take it today without even being able to speak. Agoraphobia ceases me. Some would have said that I had no choice. But I did, I could choose to keep sinking, suffering, or I choose to recover and go.

My husband (may he rest in peace) told me once: "Be careful, don't be like the cat of Mark Twain." He had jumped once on a hot stove and had burnt its belly. After that, he stopped jumping on hot stoves... But he wouldn't even jump on cold stoves.

In fact, I don't really have good memories of public transportation, but I must be careful not to let my bad experiences turn into generalities or prejudices. I must try to understand the divine pedagogy behind each one them and especially not generalise because I can choose my thoughts. This fear of the crowd and this fear or being scared are noxious weeds for my garden. I must prevent them from rooting. I will show them that I am the master of my mind and that they are not welcome in it. Each time they will show up, I will chase them away, sweep them away from my mind.

All my noble intentions and amazing projects have no value, if I don't get ready to take action. Silence and reflection during this journey will enable me to have this preparation, if God wills.

When God gave us the power to rule over the world, He also gave us the power to rule over ourselves, over our minds, so let's go, let's dare our lives!

W. Clement Stone and Napoleon Hill said in their book Success Through a positive Mental attitude: "You can do anything which doesn't go against the rules of God or of humans, provided that you are ready to pay the price for it".

Our success in this life has a price, the one of effort, the one of self-knowledge, of perseverance and control... Am I willing to pay the price?

I took my courage in my hands and went quietly, it's the rule that God imposed on me today. A rule? **It is what is imposed or adopted as a guideline. Once I arrived on the platform, I actually look at those possible lines and ways on the plan.** And there starts within me a disturbing inner dialogue. These famous projections, these lessons which give me the impression that time stops for a while.

I question myself and say: "How many of us are looking at their lives the way I am looking at this plan? How many of us are only looking at this conductor line drawn before our eyes? This clear line, which distinguishes itself so well on this multi-linear and multi-colour plan of our life choices, this plan hanging on the walls of the platforms of our day-to-day routine... We can see the line ISLAM, EMAAN, EHSAN. But we don't take this train. We don't have time and we are alone anyway.

Then there are people who wait for us, there are people who care about us, there are people who meet us every day and salute us at the stations JUDGMENTS, DEPRECIATION and IGNORANCE...We can't leave them and we hear only good things about the station ISLAM, there are so many things going on, that you might also be a bit scared, but it's not the main reason which prevents us from stopping... We live on the other side, on the opposite, too far away you know? We would have to make too many detours, too many concessions, we would have to change platforms too many times. And we work a lot, we really can't afford to do that.

Blocked standing up in this train without being able to get out at the station REVERT, REPENT, NEW WAY, NEW BEGINNING; retained from our back by the thousand and one needs and anxieties of our relatives, distressed by the sticker they had put with attention. You know the one with "Mind the gap". The one which tells us before we come out of the train, Be careful "There's a gap between God and you, don't cross the gap. Be careful, you might fall on the highway to finding your soul. Don't come out, don't say the *Shahada*... don't take the right train...

MIND THE GAP

There are some people who, suddenly out of impatience, in ultimate rebellion, despite what is written on the sticker, manage to get themselves out of the day-to-day routine, in order not to have to get out at the stations DEPRECIATION, WASTE OF TIME... As a result, they brake the chains which were retaining them until today on this train of day-to-day routine and reassuring illusions.

They extract themselves and get out a bit further, **sadly**, without having been able to experience the stations where they get out. And all of sudden, they panic, because it's not enough to get out of the train. Above all, you need to learn how to ask: **"Excuse me, which way is it? Which way is it? I want to come out of the underground or leave the platform and reach the surface."** Learn to look for the arrows... Even, sometimes, learn how to avoid them...

For some people, they have been told that there will be a family waiting for them at this station, that there will be a community to support them, but there, it's sometimes so loud that they don't even understand. BUT which way is it? Which way is it, please, to come out of the underground or leave the platform?

There are some people who manage to come out, but no one is there. They verify then that it is the right station REVERT, the station REPENT. Yes, it's the right one, it's really the station NEW BEGINNING: "But if it's really here, then where are all those who were with me on the train? I'm not the only one who came out, right? I'm not hearing voices, I'm not dreaming!!!

Separated from the ones they love, not really sure of what they're doing, they suddenly feel all alone, those who dared to come out on this platform, come out of their day-to-day train routine... with in their hearts, a deep feeling of emptiness, a deep feeling of abandonment.

There are some people who, because of their fear to go outside, because of their lack of self-confidence, of trust in others, of trust in **God**, because of their fear to go have a look at what's happening above, decide to come back to the starting point. But how will they do? The next train makes them go backwards; I can see them retracing their steps, they go further than their initial "starting point". The loud speakers shout: "Rien ne va plus! Les jeux sont faits! Everybody gets out". Where are they? What is happening to them? Everything is dark. They see a first letter, a D, then an E, then a P, then an R, then an E, then SS, and finally three letters ION. The name of this station is really long, the train had been driving for such a long time before stopping. Our day-to-day train routine therefore has DEPRESSION as terminal.

Yes, how many of us would like to be accompanied just a bit further up above the platform? Just above the station ISLAM, beyond our genealogical nature, beyond a simple sound in our name, beyond the station NORTH-AFRICAN, AFRICAN, ASIAN... way beyond, accompanied towards places where brotherhood reigns between all humans, the richness of differences, where we all share and put our ideas together, contrarily to opposing our opinions. Yes, how many of us wish that without daring to say it?

Learning how to live with ourselves and with others is without any doubt the most beautiful adventure that God is offering us in life...

But it is also the most painful, the most worrying. It is about leaving the well-known station of our day-to-day train routine, to liberate ourselves, to free ourselves from received ideas, in order to dare our life... **Dare** to be different than what the others had planned for us, in order to dare to live our choices of life, to ultimately become **actors** of our daily life.

I thought I just had to wait...

I regained control of myself, this is really where I want to go, to meet the best I can possibly be! So firstly, I need to deal with my administrative papers. The journey is long and I get on the train. I sit on the seats. On the seat right next there is a book forgotten by someone: *Tales to Heal Tales to Grow*... What an interesting title! It catches my attention... I decide to read a passage, this tale by Jacques Salomé mixes with my thoughts, deals with my thoughts.

Once upon a time, on Earth, there was a doctor, whom everyone called the Doctor of fears, also specialised in anxieties and scares. What you need to know, before we say more about it, is that on this planet Earth, all the men, all the women, and all the children had numerous fears.

Very ancient fears, coming from the depth of humanity, they would come back each time there were hardships, oblivions, lack of confidence and lack of love for God. And more recent fears coming from the childhood of every person.

In order to meet the Doctor of fears, one had to undertake a long journey of understanding, hoping to be able to iron out and erase the fears that he or she carried in her body, in his/her head or that accompanied his/her life. No one really knew how the meeting went on.

There was among those who came back from the journey a lot of modesty to share what they had experienced, how they had grown up...

One day, a child revealed the secret of the doctor of fears to those who hadn't taken the journey. But what he told them seemed so simple, so unbelievable and simple that no one believed him. He said: "He came to me, his knees against mine, he took my both hands in his and whispered to me: "Behind each fear, there is a desire. There is always a desire behind each fear, as big or as terrifying as it is. There is always a desire, be aware of it!"

"He had his mouth close to my ear and smelled like musk", said the child.

He also told me: "Behind each fear there is a desire, but also know that behind each desire there is a fear. We spend our life trying to hide our desires, that's the reason why there are so many fears in the world. And we spend our time trying to hide our fears, that's the reason why there are so many desires in the world. My one and only mission is to enable everyone to dare to understand the desires they have within them behind each of their fears."

The child, while telling all this could see that no one believed him. And he started fearing his desires and to be afraid again when he was alone. **The deceptive one had tricked them...**

One day, a man wanted to challenge the doctor of fears, he undertook the journey, came to the doctor of fears with a fear that he presented this way: "I am afraid of my desires".

The doctor of fears asked him:
"Can you tell me the scariest desire you have within you?

I have the desire to never die" replied the man.

After a long moment of silence, the doctor of fears suggested:

"And what is the fear behind this desire?"

The man replied suddenly: "I am afraid to not have the time to live my entire life for God. I am afraid to say someday: *"Ya Laytani Qadamtu li hayati" He will say: "Alas! Would that I had sent forth good deed for my life!"* (Quran, Surah 89, verse 24)

And what is the desire within you behind this fear?

I would like to live each moment of my life in the liveliest, most intense, happiest, and most pious way without wasting anything FROM it. *"Say: "Verily, my Salât (prayer), my sacrifice, my living, and my dying are for Allah, the Lord of the 'Alamîn (the worlds)"* *(Quran, Surah 6, verse 162)*

"Here is then your most redoubtable desire, the one which scares you the most", whispered the doctor of fears. "Listen to me with attention" he said. "Take care of this desire, **this is a precious and unique desire: to live each moment of my life in the liveliest, most intense, happiest, and most pious way... without wasting anything from it, this is a very beautiful desire. If you respect this desire, if you set a real PLACE in your life for it, a solid place within you, you won't fear death. Go, you can go back home."**

"O (you) the one in (complete) rest and satisfaction!
Come back to your Lord, Well-pleased (yourself) and well-pleasing (unto Him)!
Enter you, then, among My (honoured) slaves,
And enter you My Paradise!"
Surah 89, Al Fajr:

But you who are reading me, or maybe listening to me, you will surely ask me: **"Who is the doctor of fears?" You have to tell me. How and with whom do you manage to appease your fears? Do you know them? Have you ever dared to count them or speak about them? Which ones did you manage to overcome and how? Which are the ones which subsist and how? What do you think about your fears if I tell you that behind each one of them there is a hidden desire? And in this case, are you able to recognise your hidden desires?**

If everyone tried to find out the desire they have within themselves, behind every fear, we would have less fears and consequently less fears...

Yes, it's true. These questions are good. What am I afraid of? What do I desire? And what calms my fears down? What fuels them? This tale was meant for me, it is a message from God. There is no coincidence in life, I just turned my head and there, right next to me, God was calling on me.

I reached my destination, put the book back on the seat, I am sure it will benefit others.

BACK TO THE ESSENTIAL PURPOSE OF YOUR BEING

• Keep your notebook updated, do your exercises every day, it is one of the best initiatives of personal growth. This tool will help you make less errors, with the help of God and to clarify your intentions. Keeping your notebook will encourage you to think about what you do out of your days. It is a support on which you can write down your life strategies, to write all the things which you think are important to achieve a spiritual, familial and professional life of high quality. It should help you question yourself, to analyse yourself and evaluate yourself, etc. Don't forget the subtitle of this book: ***Starting from what we are to become the ideal person that we can be.***

•In order to discuss with other readers, sign in on the forum on our Facebook page: P.S.:Back to your essential heavenly being.

•**Each day, give yourself a silent moment favourable for reflection and meditation:** isolate yourself in a quiet place, sit down or lie down and cultivate the art of silence. Don't speak to anyone. Don't write. Don't read. Think as less as possible. Disengage intellectually. Imagine that your spirit is a lake and try to make it as flat as a mirror. (...) pay attention to "the voice of silence", a deep breath of beauty and harmony... **the ideal and favourable moment for that is just after the prayer of *Fajr* while waiting for the sun to rise... it's up to you.**

• Underline with a pencil the passages which touched you and copy them in your notebook while précising what touched you. Inspiring yourself from the previous chapter, draw the garden of your spirit. Which are the noxious weeds which often come to disturb you? Materialise them in your drawing.

• Dedicate one page in your notebook with the following title: **"My doubts and questions".** Start to enumerate them.

• Dedicate a few blank pages, let's say four, at the end of your notebook and write the following title: "My travel companions". You will write here all the books you have read during the year. The first book which I recommend you to read is ***If Only I'd Listen to Myself: Resolving the Conflicts That Sabotage Our Lives*** by Jacques Salomé.

• Always answer the questions in the chapter in your notebook.

• Draw the "window of your life".

• Begin the list of the **101 things you dream to accomplish before you die.**

Bonus

• Following the example of Ibn Al Jawzi, may he rest in peace, don't let your ideas fly by during the day, write them down in your notebook.

• Try and find the meaning of the hieroglyphs if you're interested.

"Courage is resistance to fear, mastery of fear, not absence of fear."

Mark Twain

Thank God, today, on Earth, I managed to overcome some of my fears: I took public transportation alone and I dealt with administrative papers at the Ministry. Pretending I had a voice extinction, I had written down what I needed. Therefore, I fought on several fronts, firstly within myself to accept my speechlessness without complaining, then on the outside against my fears and apprehensions. **Once unchained by the decisions I took,** I felt that I was doing spins within my virtuous circle. I didn't want to stop now that I was doing so well! And this wasn't just a nice intention. I know that this little victory provided me with a boost, but I know that the *Jihad against myself* is still not over. "No rest for the believer until his death", right? I have understood that the human being cannot be a temporary actor of his or her life.

On the way back, I was thinking about my life, about the things which I still need to do since he left. My notebook on my knees, I was writing, in order not to let my daily butterflies flee... Thank you Sheikh Ibn Al Jawzi (may he rest in peace)...

Apparently, for many people **the future they dream about is often just a return to their idealised past.** Me personally, I don't want to spend the rest of my life looking back. Looking at the blind spot, at the interior mirror, for my future I want to answer in the present tense... I want to lead my life forward. The second which went by doesn't belong to me anymore, the second to come doesn't belong to me yet, I want to focus on the one right now, the one I'm living.

While in the transportation or walking I listen to Quran. But I remember a very beautiful song which my beloved dedicated to me one day. It was spoken word by Grand Corps Malade. There is a passage which I will never forget. And today, it is even more striking:

I am of those who think that there are no insurmountable barriers
You just have to believe in it, as much as there are flowers which grow in the sand
And it is when you fight that there are nice victories which you can snatch
Like standing up with a backbone made of papier maché
I'm not telling you anything new, you are alive, you know how it is.
To live means accepting pain, failures and deaths
But it is also a lot of happiness, we will find it by insisting
And for that, you need heart and the mental of a resistant.
(Mental)

Heart and the mental of a resistant, yes, since then, I admitted the two principal ingredients which I will need to dose in life. I am convinced that everything my husband did before dying made sense. This sudden willingness to read loads of biographies isn't significant, it's purpose was to sustain the mental of a resistant within him. He had found a common point between the heroes of the time: "Each approach of the hero starts by defining an enemy in order to defend a cause which goes beyond him!" All these personalities, all these men and all these women had a public enemy number one. They used to sleep just a bit, eat a bit, and would never leave their eyes off him.

"God is the eternal confidant in this tragedy
In which everyone is a hero"
Charles Baudelaire
(Personal Diaries)

They resisted, fought and exposed the inacceptable, for some it was hunger, for others imperialism, injustice, inequality of opportunities... **But what about me, who are my heroes? What are my claims? On how many generations will my life make sense?** They used to fight day and night, the heart filled with love. They forbid themselves Hate, they always had hope in the human species, still filled with **certainties and convictions**. But where are mine? It has been two months since his death. **Would I be able today to defend a cause which goes beyond my daily routine? A cause which would go beyond my trials, my little scratches, my little sleep, my little work routine?**

As much as dough needs baking soda, we all need heroes, role models of excellence in order to always see further in our lives. Timeless heroes, but also more contemporary heroes, mastering speech, mastering their desires, mastering their fears, mastering their time... Some came to us **to teach us how to be and think, to be and testify, to be and hope...While some others crossed our paths to teach us how to receive, to ask, to give, to decline, to listen, to hear, to say, to deal with our sadness, our anger, our feelings of love... to teach us to speak, to transmit, to stay... to leave... to teach us to trust... to forgive, to repair, to eat, to sleep... to teach us to organise ourselves... to manage... to prioritise, to dare... to forbid ourselves from some things, to teach us to travel, to plan... to live and to die.**

I think about all these people who were there, at some point of my life, to teach me some of these lessons... before leaving. My heavy head leaning against the window, I am wondering about all these teachings, when suddenly a beggar entered the coach. I don't know if the man is so different or if I am looking at him so differently, but him entering here impressed me. Without knowing it, he was there for me, at the right time.

He reminds me that one day Gandhi, while he was going from one coach to another on a train, lost one of his clappers on the railway. The first reaction he had touched me deeply. He took his second clapper and threw it on the railway. The one accompanying him asked him: "Why did you just do that?" Gandhi answered that one clapper wouldn't be useful, he had to throw the second one so that the loss of the first one makes sense, sense for the one losing it and the one finding it... His first reaction wasn't to try and find how to get it back, or getting angry, or shout... with no shoe left? But he had the almost innate reflex to think about his neighbour... and to give meaning to his destiny.

The train of my life is now in motion, I need to take back the commands to learn again how to **have the good reflexes**. Bernard Baudouin says: ***"Wanting to change**, it is arriving at the end of a story, of a dynamic, of a project, of an experience; it is suddenly realising that you came to the end of the object of your investment; it is suddenly perceiving that in order to really move forward you need to initiate something else; it is having a feeling getting clearer and clearer that you stand in front of a wall, of an invisible limit which blocks you and prevents you from moving forward; it is having the indescribable sensation that you cannot evolve anymore in this context, that we absolutely need to get out of it in order to "grow".*

Wanting to change is also, often times, feeling that you want to be "elsewhere", do "something else", so that things move, in order to really feel that we are thriving... in one word, it is the perspective of "revival" while you actually never stop functioning, perpetuating the movement which animates us, to entertain this fabulous "machine" which serves us both as a body and a "vehicle".

Seeing this man had the effect of taking off the veil which was darkening my days. A veil which prevented me from hearing, understanding, seeing all the messages that God was putting in front of me. From now on, I want to declare around me all the **"know-how to be" and work on my reflexes.** I will defend myself and box **my bad attitudes, my bad habits**. Thank you dear stranger for this sign to me, I asked God for a beacon. He provided me with many... *"We will show them Our Signs in the universe, and in their own selves" (Quran, Surah 41, verse 53).*

Actually, I don't think that what I experienced today is much different from what I usually experience, but I know for sure that I have paid more attention than ever to the meetings, presences, thoughts, messages of my fate and destiny, and this is what allowed me to see, during this ordinary day, an extraordinary horizon through the window of my train.

"Laziness: habit of taking rest
Before being tired."
Jules Renard
(Journal)

When a habit has been settled within ourselves for too many years, we can't kick it out within one day. **You firstly need to identify it, to call it and understand how it entered in order to find out how to politely open the door for it and throw it out** and lead it to the stairs, make it go down, step by step, hand in hand, to make sure it really left. To sum it up, it needs to understand that it isn't welcome. Habits, I have loads of them, and there's more than one that I would like to see away from my door. Accepting the idea of change already means taking a step towards the stairs. It is opening myself to the possibility to see the world in a different light. **I know the secret passage, it is in my emotions...**

Once back home, I made wudu and made the mandatory prayers I missed and also the voluntary ones. I try to apply my husband's advice, bit by bit. **"Your mandatory prayers aren't enough, help yourself with voluntary prayers. They are supplementary guarantees for you. Fast and pray twelve units per day and eleven during the night. These spiritual remedies have helped many desperate hearts."** Since I received this letter, I haven't stop praying twelve units of prayer a day and eleven at night.

I pray two units of prayer before the prayer of *Fajr*, then before noon, three units of *Duha*, then at *Dhur*, I pray two units before and two after. By doing so, by mid-day, I have already obtained the rewards of a house in Paradise, by God's Grace, as the Prophet, peace and prayers be upon him, said. I think that this also helped me as I didn't have to take sedatives or sleeping pills at night.

I sent emails to my family and told them not to worry and I decided, after having eating a bit, to work on my famous habits, on these attitudes which make my life hard. I put a CD on for thinking and I took my notebook, in which I started by writing all my questions:

What are my habits, good or bad, in terms of my "know-how-to-be", in the section "Welcoming"? Do I know how to **receive?** Do I know how to welcome a gift? Do I know how to welcome a compliment? Do I know how to welcome a criticism, a remark? Do I know how to welcome a change in program in my life? Do I know how to welcome a hardship? Do I know how to welcome happiness?

Do I know how to welcome guests? Do I know how to welcome a difference of opinion? Do I know how to welcome novelty? Do I know how to welcome propositions, invitations? Do I know how to welcome for God?

What are my habits, good or bad, in terms of my "know-how-to-be", in the section "Asking"? Do I know how to **ask?** Do I know how to ask for information, advice, counsel, feedback? Do I know how to ask for a favour, a need?

Do I know how to ask or money? Do I know how to ask news from someone? Do I know how to ask for help? Do I know how to ask for love, affection, tenderness? Do I know how to ask Allah?

My husband used to tell me: "If you plan to reach a complete personal development, my beloved wife, you have to work on developing your spirituality". This section "Knowing how to ask God" will contribute to it." In order to explain this better, he made me listen to a conference of Sheikh Tariq Al Suweidan, one day when I was feeling down. My husband had become wise at the end of his life, and he could feel any sign of my malaise.

Ibn Mas'ud, may Allah be pleased with him said: "Wake up early in the morning to know how to learn or listen. Don't do anything else than knowing, learning or listening..."

When I wasn't feeling well, he wouldn't bother me with questions, no, he would take time to listen to me. On that evening, the solution he had found was to make me listen to a conference. Actually, we all know the answer, we recite the method more than seventeen times a day, without even paying attention to it. Lying on the couch, my head leaning against his shoulder, I learned how to ask, may He be Exalted, the Almighty!

In the Surah *The Opening*, the *Fatiha*, God teaches me how to ask him for something. He tells me to say and to start with *"In the Name of God, The Most Gracious, The Most Merciful"*. He expects from me that I rely on His grace and on His divine mercy. Then He asks me not to forget to praise Him, to thank Him, because He is my Master of the universe. *"Al HamduliLlahi Rabbi al 'alamine."* I thank the One who holds everything, Who masters everything, I can't find a better Listener than Him. There is no one above him to whom I could talk to. He is The First, He is the Last, I thank The Living Who never dies. *"Ar Rahman Ar Raheem"*, I testify that God is The Most Gracious, The Most Merciful. I believe in His grace and count on it on Earth and on His Mercy in the Hereafter. *"Maliki yawmi deen"*, I talk to The Sovereign, to The one who reigns and will reign on the Judgment Day. I confirm, before asking anything, one of the pillars of my faith: *my belief in the Judgment Day* and I testify that it is really Him The Only One that I worship and from Him alone comes my help.

"Iyyaka na'budu wa iyyaka nasta'een". These first five verses that God asks us to recite in all our prayers teach us how to ask something from God, the know-how for invocations.

Because it is only at the 6th verse that our request is made. And what a request! *"Guide us to the straight path", "Ihdina seerat al mustaqim"*. God tells us here: **when you ask Me, ask Me for what I am expecting from you.** God wants me to go on the straight path, so ask Him for it. God wants us to be sincere, so ask Him for it... God wants us to love His Prophets, so ask Him for it. God says: when you ask Me, ask Me for what I am expecting from you. "**Seerata ladheena an'amta aleyheem". "Guide me, O Lord, to the way of those on whom You have bestowed Your Grace".** God expects from us that we ask Him to guide us on this path. Then God says *"Ghayri al maghdudbi aleyhim walaa dhaleen"*: *"When you ask Me, ask me for protection from the path of those who deserved My Anger* (that is to say those who disobey God) *and from the path of those who went astray* (those who deny the existence of God and the pillars of faith)". God taught us to ask Him. May God answer our invocations and may He help us apply His method. Ameen! Learning how to ask Allah is part of the pathway for all those who strive for an ideal version of themselves...

This evening, I keep loudly and clearly writing in my notebook... **What are my good or bad habits in terms of my "know-how-to-be", in the section "Giving"?** Do I know how to Give? Do I know how to give a present? Do I know how to give a compliment, encouragements? Do I know how to give a critic, a remark? Do I know how to give happiness?

Do I know how to give my opinion without vexing or offending someone? Do I know how to give an invitation, an information, an opinion, an advice, a feedback? Do I know how to give a service, to answer a need? Do I know how to give personal involvement? Do I know how to give money? Do I know how to give my time? To give my knowledge? Do I know how to give news?

Do I know how to give help? Do I know how to give love, affection and tenderness? Do I know how to give for the sake of God? **Do I know how to give myself to God?** My husband used to remind me often that the word *Islam* means in Arabic "Giving yourself entirely to God". If I say that I am a Muslim, I am supposed to convince myself to dedicate my heart, my body and my soul, entirely to God. Is it the case? Do I entirely devote myself to Him? Are my intentions, while dealing with social and family matters, totally dedicated to Him? Ouch! These questions hurt...

What are my habits, good or bad, in terms of my "know-how-to-be", in the section "Refusing"? Do I know how to refuse? Do I know how to refuse a proposition? Do I know how to refuse help? Do I know how to refuse for the sake of God? Do I tend to refuse too many things to myself?

What are my habits, good or bad, in terms of my "know-how-to-be", in the section "Listening"? Do I know how to listen? Do I know how to **listen** without speaking? Do I know how to listen with empathy to someone **who speaks** without focusing on the topic of the discussion? Do I know how to listen to my parents? Do I know how to listen to my husband? Do I know how to listen to my children? Do I know how to listen to divine advice? Do I know how to listen to the signs?

What are my habits, good or bad, in terms of my "know-how-to-be", in the section "Waiting"? Do I know how to **wait?** Do I know how to wait for a change? To wait or happiness? Do I know how to wait for information? To wait for a service, a need? Do I know how to wait for something from God?

What are my habits, good or bad, in terms of my "know-how-to-be", in the section "Saying"? Do I know how to **say?** Do I know how to say the truth wisely, truly and calmly? Do I know how to say to my family this is my true self? To my husband? To my children? Do I know how not to say?

I was told that the function of sadness is, contrarily to what we think, to help someone bear an emotional pain, a disappointment, when it is measured and sound... For me, sadness has provoked a loss of energy, a lack of enthusiasm for activities in this life, especially for distractions and pleasures. **In reality, this withdrawal from other and social activities, going back within myself** was something God wanted, in order to enable me to mourn, to digest the deceived hopes and to evaluate the consequences on my own life.

Because he hasn't left me long in that state, he has been infusing a new energy within me for a few days, an energy stronger than the sadness and more fair, which will project me forward towards new latitudes... new habits!

What are my habits, good or bad, in terms of my "know-how-to-be", in the section "Dealing with my sadness"? Do I know how to **deal** with my sadness? Alone or with my family? To my mind, are there reasons which don't justify sadness? Do I know how to identify against whom and for what I am really sad? To my mind, is it possible to control the feeling of sadness? How can I be sad without it affecting my faith? My health? My relatives? But what is it actually, that makes me sad? And what calms my sadness?

What are my habits, good or bad, in terms of my "know-how-to-be", in the section "Deal with my anger"? Do I know how to **deal** with my anger? Alone or with my family? To my mind, are there reasons which don't justify anger? Do I know how to identify against whom and for what I am really angry? To my mind, is it possible to control my anger? How can I be angry without it affecting my faith? My health? My relatives? But what is it actually which makes me angry? And what calms my anger?

When I think about the times I was angry, I always remember the verse: *"And remember Dhun-Nûn (Jonah), when he went off in anger, and imagined that We shall not punish him! But he cried through the darkness saying:* ***Lâ ilâha illa Anta [none has the right to be worshipped but You (O Allâh)], Glorified are You. Truly, I have been of the wrong-doers!"*** *So We answered his call, and delivered him from the distress. And thus We do deliver the believers"* (Quran, Surah 21, verse 88). I know that in order to fight against my anger and reach the ideal version of myself, I absolutely need to make *Dhikr*.

Since my husband's death, I have followed his advice and I have committed myself to a *Wird* (spiritual program), a minimum of reminders. **I say 100 times "Astaghfirullah", 300 times "Allahumma salli wa sallam 'ala Nabiyyina Muhammad", peace and blessings be upon him and 1000 times "La Illaha illa Allah"** every day. I have a manual counter which is very useful for this.

Every evening, before sleeping, I read the Surah *Al Fatiha*, with the required focus and understanding, I hope. I ask God to guide me to the straight path, I ask Him to let me enter the path full of light in order to progress towards excellence and divine satisfaction. I ask Him for love, interconnection and communication of the pious souls with each other like when we do it at the moment of the ***Tahiyaat***, an important step of the prayer...

Then I read the **Surahs Al Kafirun and Al Ikhlas**, through which I reaffirm my Tawheed, the bases of my faith and I separate my path from that of the people who deserve God's wrath. Finally, to be accompanied during this spiritual journey, I send prayers upon the Prophet Muhammad, peace and blessings be upon him, because he is the best of intercessors.

Finally, I start my evening invocation which my husband has taught me. This invocation brings the hearts of the believers together.

In The Name of God, The Most Gracious, The Most Merciful

"My Lord, I send my salutations *to the Angels who surround me, creatures of light that You honoured by the fact that they never disobey you. Make them love my house and my company on Earth and in the Hereafter. O Lord, send my salutations to them,* **to all the Angels named in the Quran and those which I don't know about.** *Send my salutations to* **the Angels carrying the Throne** *(Surah 40, verse 7) and allow me to be among those who love each other for the sake of Allah on the Day of Resurrection, protected under the shade of Your Throne. On the day when there will be no shade but the shade of Your Throne. Salutations to* **the scribe Angels**, *(Surah 83, verse 10-12). O my Lord, may the book of my deeds be the most filled and the heaviest on the Day of Accounting. Salutations to* **the guardian Angels** *(Surah 6, verse 61) and don't leave me alone at any moment, without the beneficial company of these angels. Salutations to* **the Angel of death**, *(Surah 32, verse 11). My Lord, may he come to me in his best appearance. Alleviate my suffering at the time of my death and make it a relief. Salutations to* **the Angel Michael,** *who is in charge of distributing the goods to each one of us.*
My Lord, make him come visit me often if it is beneficial to me. Salutations to **the Angel Ridwan**, *Chief of the guardians of Paradise.*

Ya Rabb, allow me to meet him and to be welcomed by him in Paradise. Salutations to **the Angel Malik**, *Chief of the guardians of Hell. O Lord, may I not appear on his list.*

Salutations to **Munker and Naker**, *in charge of questioning us in the grave. O Lord, may they come to me in their best appearance, may they count me among those who used to do a review every evening on Earth and who already have the answers.*

Salutations to **the Angel Gabriel**, *who is believed to have six hundred wings. His missions are each more beautiful than the last. May God grant me his help on the bridge of Sirat. Salutations to* **the Angel who is going to blow the trumpet**. *May God resurrect me in a state of prostration and may He preserve me from the trials on the Day of Accounting.*

My Lord, you have sent more than **124,000 prophets** *and You remain The Most Knowledgeable. I ask You to send my salutations to all of them, and to have the opportunity to be with them in Paradise to hear them telling me their different missions.*

Salutations, O my Lord, to **my father Adam, peace and blessings be upon him and to my mother Hawa, peace be upon her.** *May God allow me to be with them in Paradise, may He make them proud of me and may He fill my heart with sincere love for them. May He provide me with their vision in my dreams. May He protect me from the jealous people as was Cain towards his brother Abel. And may He count me among the pious offspring of Adam and Eve. Finally, salutations to their son* **Seth,** *peace and blessings be upon him, who also was a prophet.*

Peace and blessings on **our Prophet Idriss**, *peace and blessings be upon him. May Allah allow me to visit him on the 4th floor of His Paradise, may He make him proud of me for the usage of the quill (pen) and Knowledge, and may He fill my heart with sincere love for him. May God allow me to have the company of the Angel on Earth like him, and may He provide me with the vision of this prophet in my dreams.*

Salutations to **our Prophet Nuh,** *peace and blessings be upon him. May Allah allow me to meet him in Paradise, may He make him proud of me for my determination on Earth to transmit the message of the oneness of God. May God save me and count me among the sincere people and preserve me from* **natural disasters** *like He saved His prophet Nuh from the deluge, peace and blessings be upon him. May He prevent me from having a son who disobeys to the message like Yam did with his father. May*

He fill my heart with sincere love for this Prophet and provide me with his vision and advice in my dreams.

Salutations to **our Prophet Hud**, *peace and blessings be upon him. May God enable me to meet him in Paradise, may He make him happy to meet me in the Hereafter. May God save me and protect me* **from droughts**, *like He saved His Prophet Hud, peace and blessings be upon him and his followers. May He preserve me from being like the people of 'Ad. May* **God protect me from devastating winds, from the cold and the ice.** *May He fill my heart with sincere love for this Prophet and provide me with his vision in my dreams.*

Salutations to **our Prophet Saleeh**, *peace and blessings be upon him. May Allah enable me to meet him in Paradise, may He make him satisfied with me when he meets me in the Hereafter. May God save me and protect me from His anger, as He saved His Prophet Saleeh, peace and blessings be upon him, and his followers. May He prevent me from resembling the people of Thamud. May God protect me from earthquakes and thunder. May He fill my heart with sincere love for this Prophet and grant me his vision in my dreams.*

Prayers and salutations on **our Prophet Ibraheem**, *peace and blessings be upon him. Salutations and peace to his sons* **Ismaeel and Isaaq.** *May Allah enable me to meet them and be with them in Paradise, may God grant me their numerous qualities. May He also make me among those who do good and are merciful, being caring and kind to my parents. May Allah grant me high intelligence which will allow me, during my entire life, to condemn the evil and advise the good, with the best rhetoric to the highest parts of governments.*
May God grant me sincerity and good fate and may He inspire respect for me in the hearts of people. And God is sufficient for me, He is The Best Guardian. O my Lord, allow me to feel within me peace and coolness, on the Day of Resurrection, like You saved our Prophet Ibraheem, peace and blessings be upon him.

May God fill my heart with the same patience, certitude and trust in God that **my Sister Hajar**, *peace be upon her, when she was abandoned in the desert with her son Ismaeel. O Lord, I might have my offspring on the land of the disbelievers, far away from Your close house, the Kaaba. O Lord, make my children Arabic speakers, readers of the Quran, observers of the prayers and of the fast of the month of Ramadan, may they pay the Zakaah and accomplish their Hajj. Make them sympathetic to the people. Provide them with lawful food and maintain them on the straight path. Ya Rabb, allow them and allow us to go on pilgrimage together and to drink Zam Zam water. Allow us to visit The Holy House and to kiss the black stone, surrounded by 70,000 of Your Most beautiful Angels. May God fill my heart with sincere love for these Prophets, for whom I send my benedictions at each prayer and may He grant me with their vision and advice in my dreams.*

Salutations to **our Prophet Loot**, *peace and blessings be upon him. May God enable me to meet him in Paradise, may He make him happy to meet me in the Hereafter. May God save me and protect me* **from volcanic eruptions** *and natural disasters resulting from His anger, like He saved his Prophet Loot, peace and blessings be upon him, and his two daughters. May He preserve me and protect my offspring from the behaviour of the people of Sodom and those who followed them. May God fill my heart with sincere love for this Prophet and may He grant me and inspire me the goodness of his advice to fight the spreading of vice.*

Salutations to **our Prophet Shuaib**, *peace and blessings be upon him. May God enable me to meet him in Paradise, may He make him proud of me. May God save me and protect me from* **the dryness of the heart, the drought of Dhikr and intense heat** *resulting from His anger, like he saved His Prophet Shuaib, peace and blessings be upon him. May He preserve me and protect my offspring from the behaviour of the people of Madyan and those who followed them. May God fill my heart with sincere love for this Prophet and may He grant me and inspire me with the goodness of his advice to fight the spreading of heedlessness and forgetfulness.*

Salutations to **our Prophets Ya'qub**, *peace and blessings be upon him,* **and Yussuf,** *peace and blessings be upon him. May God allow me to meet them and be with them in Paradise. May God grant me their numerous qualities. May God preserve me from jealousy within our families and in the societies we live in.*

And God is sufficient for us, He is The Best Guardian. O my Lord, allow me to have nice dreams and have the best interpretations. Give me the best friends. And make that the people around us admire our noble character, our sincere faith, our actions, our words, the worship we have for You, our charity, until they testify Your Oneness. May God fill my heart with the same patience, certitude and trust in God as these two Prophets.

Salutations to **our Prophet Ayyub**, *peace and blessings be upon him. May God save me and protect me from hardships which would take me away from His Reminders and His Mention. May He preserve me and my offspring from incurable diseases. May He make me from among the worthy and devoted spouses like the wife of our Prophet Ayyub, peace and blessings be upon him. May God fill my heart with sincere love for this Prophet and his wife and may He grant me and inspire me with the goodness of his advice to fight weakness and heedlessness in hardships.*

Salutations to **our Prophet Yunus**, *peace and blessings be upon him. May God allow me to meet him in Paradise, may He make him proud of me and my offspring. May God save me and* **protect me against the hardships and disasters on Earth, in the sea, in the night as well as in the day.** *May He answer my prayers as much as He answered our Prophet Yunus' prayers, peace and blessings be upon him, and saved him. O my Lord, I beg You like Yunus begged You from the belly of the wale. Count me among the repenting people and grant me Your mercy and be pleased with my husband's soul. O Lord, enable me to remain faithful to You and enable me to remember You in times of ease and hardship.*

May God fill my heart with sincere love for this Prophet and may He allow me to meet the people who were fortunate to be guided by him in Paradise and may He grant me his companionship and his vision in my dreams.

Salutations to **our Prophet Musa,** *peace and blessings be upon him,* **and his brother Harun,** *peace and blessings be upon him. Ya Rabb, protect me like you protected Musa from the claws of Pharaoh. Grant me the same reliance on God (Haqq Al Yaqin) as the Prophet Musa, peace and blessings be upon him, when he took his stick and pointed it at the sea and protect me from the ingratitude and the attitude that the people worshiping the calf towards Harun. O my Lord enable me to be with* **Assya**, *peace and blessings be upon her, in Your high heaven, allow me to be among her close neighbours at Your side. Grant my brothers and sisters who don't have children yet with children like you granted Musa, peace and blessings be upon him, to Assya.*

O my Lord, put Your Barakah in the milk of my sisters who are breastfeeding their child like You did for the milk which our prophet drank during his nursing. O Lord, enable me to apply Your commandments, which you revealed to Musa, not to commit perjury, to be nice to my parents, neither to kill nor to harm innocents. ***Preserve me from adultery and keep me away from anything that resembles it. Protect me from the desire to steal and robbers. Protect me from false testimony, allow me to have nice neighbours on earth and in the Hereafter. Alive and in my grave, awake and asleep.*** *Protect me from jealousy and envy, from Shirk and allow me to become wise like You did for Your close slave* **Al Khidr**. *Grant me the companionship of people who will remind me of You... O my Lord, render the use of witchcraft impotent on us and put between us and the magicians a protecting veil, like You enabled Musa's stick to swallow the magicians' snakes. Protect me from Your wrath and from the calamities which come from it. May God fill my heart with sincere love for our Prophet Musa, peace and blessings be upon him, and his brother, peace and blessings upon him, may He enable me to meet them in Paradise and may He grant me the companionship and their vision in my dreams.*

Salutations to **our Prophet Ilyas**, *peace and blessings be upon him, may God grant me with his companionship in Paradise. May He preserve me from the behaviour of the worshipers of Bal and may He save me like He saved the worshipers of the unique God.*

Salutations to **our Prophets Alyasa**, *peace and blessings be upon him,* **and Samuel,** *peace and blessings be upon him, descendants of Harun, the brother of Musa, may God make me someone close to them in Paradise. May God fill my heart with sincere love for these Prophets, may He enable me to know them better and to meet them in Paradise. May He grant me their companionship and their vision in my dreams.*

Salutations to **our Prophet Dawud (David)**, *peace and blessings be upon him, may God make me one of his neighbours in Paradise. O my Lord! You granted our prophet Dawud, peace and blessings be upon him, with the most beautiful voice with which he used to recite Your Praises. O Lord, allow me to praise you in the most beautiful way and allow me to hear the voice of your Prophet Dawud, peace and blessings be upon him, in my dreams and in the Hereafter. May my voice join the birds singing when I recite Your sacred words in the Quran. And help me in the learning of the beauty of Tajweed. May the prophet Dawud join me in my grave, once I am dead, and grant me his companionship as well as his most beautiful recitation of Your revealed words. O Lord, strengthen our faith like you strengthened our prophet Dawud's faith, peace and blessings be upon him, improve and increase my fasting like You beautified the fasting of Dawud, allow me to be like him, full of deference for You. Make me live in harmony with nature and the animals.*

And grant me **wisdom and the art of resolving disputes.** *May God fill my heart with sincere love for this Prophet Dawud, peace and blessings be upon him), may He allow me to meet him in Paradise and in my grave and may He grant me the hearing of his psalmody in my dreams.*

Salutations to **our Prophet Salomon (Suleyman)**, *peace and blessings be upon him, may God make me someone close to him in Paradise. O Lord, answer my supplication* *which is the one Your Prophet Salomon, peace and blessings be upon him, made to You: "Lord, inspire within sincere gratitude for the blessing that You are granting us and may all our actions be pleasing to You. Count us among the just thanks to Your Mercy. Amine." O Lord, grant me a great favour close to You and grant me a beautiful offspring and a good fate. May God fill my heart with sincere love for this Prophet, may He allow me to meet him in Paradise ad may He grant me with his vision in my dreams.*

Salutations to **our Prophets Zakariya**, *peace and blessings be upon him,* **and his son Yahya,** *peace and blessings be upon him, may God count me among their guests in Paradise. Kaf, ha, ya 'Ayn, Saad, I mention the sign of goodness that God gave to Zakariya. O Lord, You who says to something be and it is, I don't despair of Your Mercy. Grant my sterile brothers and sisters with a good posterity and a pious offspring like You answered the invocation of our Prophet Zakariya, peace and blessings be upon him, with his son Yahya.*

O Lord, You who knows the pure hearts and hears the secret voices, You say in Your Sacred Book: "Zakariya, Yahya, Issa and Ilyas, all of them known for their virtue". Lord, fill our hearts with their virtues and impregnate our acts with their behaviour. O my Lord, grant our children wisdom from an early age, like You did for our Prophet Yahya, peace and blessings be upon him, from his childhood. Ya Rabb, assist them on the day of their birth, of their death and of their resurrection. May God fill my heart with sincere love for these Prophets, may He enable me to know them better and to meet them in Paradise. May He grant me their companionship and their visions in my dreams.

Salutations to **our Prophet Jesus (Issa)**, *peace and blessings be upon him, may God count me among this companions in Paradise. O Lord, You chose Adam, Nuh, the offspring of Ibrahim and the one of the family of 'Imran among all human beings. All these chosen ones form one single lineage, O Lord, count me among the pious people of this virtuous lineage. O Lord, you chose* **Mary (Maryam) the mother of**

***Jesus** as the Head of the women in Paradise, may I be among the people close to her. O Lord, I invoke you with the words of Issa who said: "Despite Your greatness, You are close and despite Your closeness, You are eminent. You are above everything that You created, O Lord, count me among the grateful people and those who know You." Our Prophet Issa, peace and blessings be upon him, used to speak but to say good words, otherwise he would stay quiet. O Lord, enable me to use words only within Your Light and **preserve me from slander, backbiting and useless speech...** May God fill my heart with sincere love for this Prophet, may He enable me to meet him in Paradise as well as his mother, may He grant me his vision and his advice in my dreams.*

*Prayers and salutations to **our beloved Prophet Muhammad**, peace and blessings be upon him, may God allow me to be from community for the eternity. May He grant me with his qualities, may He water me with His Science through His Sunna and His revealed words. O Lord, he was the trustworthy, make me from the sincere worshippers and the honest people who will be reunited with him. Allow me to drink from the Prophet's hands, peace and blessings be upon him, from the Tasneem, which is as fresh as camphor, tastes like ginger and smells like musk. The Muslim community will be the first one to drink from it, allow me to be among them. The Prophet Muhammad, peace and blessings be upon him, was a walking Quran, a mercy for humanity. O Lord, despite my shortcomings, make me **a mercy to humanity and count me among the best spokes people for this noble Prophet.** Count me among the men and the women who memorised Your sacred words which he transmitted. O Lord, we live in a society of bad customs, many people don't know the real nobility of the character of our Beloved. Protect his reputation and his honour through us.*

May we and our offspring be the best standard-bearers of Islam. O Lord, revitalize my faith, count me among Your faithful people and prevent all my senses from disobeying You. Make me live in the appropriate balance between the Hope for Your Mercy and the Fear of Disappointing You. The Prophet Muhammad, peace and blessings be upon him, was the Gatherer, may I always be a good intermediary. Lord, allow me with Your mercy to be among the people close to him in Paradise.

Ya Rabb, fill my heart with sincere love for the Prophet Muhammad, peace and blessings be upon him, fill my heart with the love of the Hereafter and protect me from the worries of this life which would bring me away from You. My Lord, help me in taking the right decisions, those which our Prophet Muhammad, peace and blessings be upon him, would have taken. May my tongue constantly salute him and pray for him and his offspring. Grant me his vision and his advice in my dreams. Honour me with his presence at all the key moments in my life. Lord, I ask You for all the good things which the Prophet, peace and blessings be upon him, asked you for and I ask You for protection against all the bad things from which Muhammad, peace and blessings be upon him, asked for Your protection.

My Lord, give my salutations to the **Mothers of the Believers** *and the spouses of our beloved Prophet Muhammad, peace and blessings be upon him. Salutations to* **Khadija**, *may God be pleased with her. May He allow us to have the same place in the hearts of our husbands as that of Khadija in the Prophet's heart, peace and blessings be upon him.*

May He enable us to have such a good reputation in this life and in the Hereafter. O Lord, grant us a place close to her in Paradise. Ameen. Salutations to **Qasim, Tayeb, Tahir, Zeyneb, Ruqaya, Um Kaltum and Fatima, the children of the Prophet,** *peace and blessings upon him, from Khadika. May God enable me to be among them all as well as with his son* **Ibraheem**, *in His highest heaven. Ameen. May God fill my heart with sincere love for the Prophet's family, may He enable me to meet him in Paradise and may He grant me the blessing of their vision in my dreams.*

O Lord, I conclude with this invocation which links the hearts to which You have granted Your blessings, and I strive for Excellence, for my best self and for Your Pleasure. May this invocation be a spiritual process which will allow me to interconnect and communicate with the pious souls, on Earth as well as in the Hereafter, awake as well as asleep. Salutations to my husband and grant me his vision in my dreams. Ameen."

This is the prayer which I make every evening before going to sleep. It helps me manage my emotions and feel the presence of God and his Prophets. Through this, I always feel protected and in good company... I imposed this spiritual exercise on myself as my husband used to do, knowing that one can't pretend to tend for the ideal person one wants to be without setting a ***wird*** and holding on to it.

It's like an athlete who would like to register to participate to the Olympic Games. Knowing this, he or she will train twice more and will regularly exercise in order to improve his or her results before the selections. It is the same for someone who is striving for the ideal version of himself or herself. We must compel ourselves to spiritual exercises, among others, in order to develop and access sound and authentic **knowledge** and **self-control**. We shouldn't forget that God is The One Who Selects.
In order to continue my research to know myself better, I need to keep studying my habits, my "know-how-to-be" in the section **"Managing the feeling of love".** Do I know how to manage my feeling of love? Alone or with my family? To my mind, are there reasons which justify the absence of love? Am I able to identify what I love and why I love it? To my mind, is it possible to manage my feelings of love? How can I love without harming my faith? My health? My relatives? By the way, what is it which makes me love?

What are my habits, good or bad, in terms of my "know-how-to-be", in the section "Trust"? Do I know how to **trust?** Do I know how to trust without talking about it? Do I know how to trust my parents? Do I know how to trust my husband? Would I know how to trust my children? Do I know how to **trust God?** And my fate? Do I know how to trust signs?

"About the reconciliation with oneself, about the meaning of forgiving".

Michel Odoul

What are my habits, good or bad, in terms of my "know-how-to-be", in the section "Forgiving"? Do I know how to **forgive?** Do I know how to forgive without speaking about it? Do I know how to forgive my parents? Do I know how to forgive my husband? Would I know how to forgive my children? Do I know how to ask for forgiveness? Do I know how to ask God for forgiveness?

What are my habits, good or bad, in terms of my "know-how-to-be", in the section "Eating"? Do I know how to **eat?** Alone or with my family? To my mind, would there be reasons to skip a meal? Not to eat? To eat too much? Do I eat to live or do I live to eat? To my mind, is it possible to control my hunger? How can I eat without affecting my faith, my worship? My health? My relatives? By the way, what are my needs in terms of food?

What are my habits, good or bad, in terms of my "know-how-to-be", in the section "Sleeping"? Do I know how to **sleep?** Alone or with my family? To my mind, would there be reasons for me not to sleep? To sleep too much? How can I tell when I am sleepy? Is it possible to control my need of sleep? How can I sleep without it affecting my faith, my worship? My health? My relatives? By the way, what are my needs in terms of sleep?

What are my habits, good or bad, in terms of my "know-how-to-be", in the section "Forbidding"? Do I know how to **forbid things to myself?** Alone or with my family? To my mind, are there reasons for which I shouldn't forbid anything to myself? Forbid too many things to myself? How do I know if I should forbid something to myself? To my mind, is it possible to control myself? How can I forbid anything to myself without it affecting my faith, my worship? My health? My relatives? By the way, what are the things which I should forbid to myself?

What are my habits, good or bad, in terms of my "know-how-to-be", in the section "Allowing"? Do I know how to **allow myself to do some things?** Alone or with my family? To my mind, are there reasons for which I shouldn't allow myself to do some things? To allow myself too many things? How do I know if I should allow myself to do something? How can I allow myself to do something without it affecting my faith, my worship? My health? My relatives? By the way, what can I allow myself to do?

"The body is a tool to communicate with us as well as with the others. The body speaks. It translates our secret emotions, our hidden desires but also our resentments, our refusals, our fears, our pains."

Professor E. Zarifian

This evening, I am tense, my eyes are burning and closing after these questions. I feel that it isn't going to be that easy to work on my habits. But I know this will help me learn how to know myself better. I will be able to start from what I am to finally become, with the help of God, the ideal I want to become and can become. As I develop my conscience, I realise how my body has stored tensions. A cramp made my calf tense so hard that I screamed out of pain... It only took one page of writing and waiting for answers about my habits to feel my body tense again stronger. This symptom is a message coming from my unconsciousness.

It is my tender mum who taught me how to capture pains in words. She studied this science from Michel Odoul, the author of ***Our body speaks, and we must know how to listen to it...*** She enabled me to understand and hear what my little daily pains are saying before they express themselves with more violence and make me lose some precious time. When my back expresses itself through the tongue of the beginning of a lumbago, it is sometimes because it is tired, or carries too much...

If my skin or my scalp is itchy, this means that something is bothering me... When my eyes talk to me through the language of repetitive sties and conjunctivitis it might be because there is something which I can't see or don't want to see. When my stomach starts singing the letter "A", with no food reason, this means that there is something which I can't digest, or which doesn't pass...

If I don't call on the positive and alert thinking, on my faith and on action to remove all these inner tensions, they would remain here and pile up on top of all the previous tensions, on top of all the nods in my thoughts, gradually transforming my body into a refuge for chronic disorders and diseases. In vain would I cure the symptoms, they won't go until I find the right answers. Once an event is finished, I need to move on, with a willingness coming from my spirit which will reason my body, my heart and my soul. As a result, **I would protect the intimate link existing between my immune system and my psyche.**

I try to shout again from my bed, to make a sound of pain come out, but in vain, nothing comes out. Even though I managed this evening to write loud and clear in my notebook, even though I already understood what this silence allowed me to do today, I still wonder about tomorrow. I can still hear my husband, if he were here he would have said: **"Speech** is incarnated language. In other words, it is the act of a subject. God took speech away from you, but what do you take out of it?

What do you hear and what do you read when you write and break down the work "speech", "parole" in French? There is the negation "pas", which means "no" and the word "role". The divine message is clear, this trial is here to encourage you to **review your roles and your responsibilities in life...** Good night and sleep well my love..." Here is what I think he would have told me today!

BACK TO THE ESSENTIAL PURPOSE OF YOUR BEING

• Underline with a pencil the passages which struck you in the whole document and copy them in your notebook, especially writing down what touched you.

• Inspiring yourself from this chapter answer the following question: "But who are my heroes? What are my claims?"

• Inspiring yourself from this passage, answer the following questions: "Would I be able today to defend a cause which is beyond my day-to-day routine? A cause which would be beyond my trials, my small body ailments, my small naps, my small jobs?" You will present the cause which is dear to you in your notebook and explain why.

• The hero says that she wants to box her bad habits, what about you? Examine all your bad habits within 24 hours. In a typical day, enumerate those bad habits and for each one of them think about a good habit which could come and replace it.

- Make sure you answer in your notebook all the questions about good and bad habits in terms of "know-how-to-be" and in the different sections (Knowing how to: welcome, ask, give, etc).

- Start to reflect and write down in your notebook, about the wird (spiritual programme) that you want to implement this year. The most important isn't the quantity, it is regularity.

- In your notebook again dedicate a few pages to the following subject: "My health and what I can say about it." Reflect and meditate about the state of your body.

- Keep listing "Your doubts and questions".

- Keep listing "the 101 things that you dream to do before you die".

Bonus

- Read the third part of the book by Michel Odoul *Dis moi où tu as mal: Je te dirai pourquoi* (Editions Albin Michel).

"Our society, our education and also a certain ease lead us to look for the satisfaction of our desires on and towards the outside. Therefore, we learn how to manage, master, dominate, possess or communicate with this outside. This crazy race takes us away from ourselves day by day and empties us from our own substance. Only death or illness bring us back before ourselves, by obligation and by force. At that moment, we are in great turmoil."

Michel Odoul (Founder of the French Institute of Shiatsu).

My husband always advised me to read, read and read again any kind of author, any theme, any document from the prism of Islam, but also from that of my understanding, in order to separate the wheat from the chaff, while drawing here and there that which could nourish and enrich my destiny, that which could speak to me... I definitely don't have the same spirituality as Michel Odoul, neither the idea he has about the hereafter, nor the meaning he gives to the body pains linked with the bruises of the soul. I am in fact convinced that the modern and fragmented medicine should have never separated our body from our soul. Yes, the oriental medicine is right, when it says that some diseases are screams from our body, messages to our soul, but not all of them are.

This evening, I'm falling asleep with calf cramps because I know that my soul is fed up with my bad habits. The pains, the tensions of the lower-limb are linked to our implication in life, to our decision making, to our supposed inabilities. This evening, this calf pain wants to let me know that I have difficulty accepting change, difficulty moving and "moving forward".

This cramp is also a sign of poor energy flow in my body. If I were a tree it would correspond to a poor flow of sap, from my roots to my top. This means I have difficulty making things come true (trunk = present, branches = future), this "willing willingness" within me, these resolutions, these ideas, these projects which are dear to my soul, dear to my body. It is hardly a new problem, but today is the time for me to solve it. Albert Camus used to say: *"True generosity towards the future consists in giving our all to what is present."*

To calm my pain, I will make wudu again and go to bed... I make sure I put my notebook on the bedside table. I set my alarm for the night prayer, one hour before *Fajr* prayer, I make my *adhkar* (invocations), then sleep on the right after having recited the *Shahada*, the profession of faith.

"Never start anything for which you would have to repent later on. Never do anything which you don't understand; but learn all that which you ought to know, and by that means you will lead a pleasant life."

Pythagore

(Extract from Golden Verses)

I wake up for the last third of the night with no cramp left, thank God. I haven't dreamed of anything in particular. I hope I will be able to speak today. But I realise that I still have that strange feeling in my mouth and that my voice still seems buried. I don't know if it is going to last three days like in the prophecy, but I pray, I pray eleven units of prayer then prepare some food. Today is Thursday and I am fasting, like every Mondays and Thursdays and the 13th, 14th and 15th of the Muslim lunar calendar. My husband used to fast once every two days, as our Prophet Dawud used to do, peace and blessing upon him. For now, I am not able to do so. But I am determined to do it one day... and to write it in my notebook.

Sitting on my prayer mat, I am waiting for the alarm clock to ring. I clear my mind, cultivate the art of silence, I intellectually start my day by Dhikr. Every morning, I try to follow the advice of a wise Tibetan about excellence: *"Sit with all the immutable and unshakeable majesty of the mountain. Let your spirit rise, emerge and hover in the air".* Once the call of the muezzin resounded, I prayed my *Sunnah* prayer then *Fajr*.

Finally, I read my daily ration of Quran, twenty-two pages. I prefer doing it on this early hour, because nothing and nobody can interrupt me... I go back to bed because I am tired. Thank God, my schedule allows me to do so today.

I wake up two hours later. My objective today is to box my bad habits and to establish a new routine in my notebook... Pythagoras used to say: "Isn't the start the beginning of everything?"

MORNING ROUTINE

Firstly, to be able to easily include my twelve units of prayers in my daily programme, I need to set new routines, starting from when I wake up:

• Undo the bed, shake the pillows and the sheets... and ventilate by opening the window.

• Take a quick shower.

• Do my wudu.

• Brush my teeth and remembering to close the tube of toothpaste.

• Clean the sink after I'm done and wipe the splashes on the mirror.

• Get dressed, do the bed.

• Put my pyjamas in their right place.

• Check if I need to do some laundry.

• Comb my hair.

• Pray Dhuha* prayer (3 times 2 units of prayer), because I noticed that if I don't do it straight after waking up, I postpone it and end up doing 14 units of prayer at Dhuhr time: Dhuha + 2 units of prayer before Dhuhr + the mandatory prayer of Dhuhr + 2 units of prayer after. This often daunts me and disturbs my attention.

• Have a balanced breakfast.
• Sweep.

To be completed.

"If you overcome yourself you have strength"
Lao Tzu

A house quickly becomes a mess if we don't have the right habits. I keep on writing in my notebook my routines for noon.

NOON ROUTINE

• Before noon, verify which areas have dust on them, dust them if necessary.
• Have a look at areas with microbes, a bit of bleach spray, hand brush and everything is clean.
• There are also areas which I call bazaar areas, areas which give you the blues. These are areas which, even clean, attract the mess because of their location... If I put a paper or clothes in these areas, then others come like magnets and accumulate... In my house, the risk zones are wardrobes, drawers, cupboards, the ironing board, the little table in the hall... and the little boxes everywhere. I finally decided to check and clean up one area by day!
• Then there are these famous things which I don't get rid of. Those which unnecessarily clutter up the house, which inevitably clutter up my thoughts, my vision. In Feng-Shui, the art of wellbeing at home, it is advised to find 27 things to throw away every day in order to clear your environment. It's silly, but it works. In order to be Zen, I need to clean from A to Zen... and throw useless things in the bin!
• When I have lunch, I won't leave the dishes for later. And pow, I fight procrastination

(the fact of postponing things to tomorrow, which you could do right now).

• I need to throw away what needs to be thrown away. I won't leave the yoghurt cup outside the bin or other garbage.

• Brush my teeth after each meal. If I am outside, I will think about carrying my Siwak in my bag.

• I won't wait until the bin is full to take it downstairs.

• I must sort the food in my fridge and I shouldn't wait until things perish.

• When I leave the house, I must think about turning on my Quran reader in the house. It is a good thing to have the Surah "The Cow" read in your house at least once every three days.

• When I take the mail upstairs, I should sort it out straight away. I can use the box I bought for this purpose.

• In the hall, every pair of shoe is at the right place in the cupboard. From now on, my coats will all be hung.

To be completed...

AFTERNOON ROUTINE:

Like some say "Sport yourself well!!!" I must absolutely set a time for sports during my day. When I am at home, the afternoon seems to be the best moment. I have a treadmill which is used as a coat hanger. I don't want this fantastic tool to testify against me in the Hereafter. "I was there, in your house, but you ignored me to the detriment of your health... You could have used me, but you didn't think about me..."

"Sports consists in delegating to the body some of the strongest virtues of the soul."

Jean Giraudoux

• We all enjoy winning, but rare are those who enjoy training. Therefore, starting from today, I will force myself to exercise a bit, even if it's only for 15 minutes per day. This will enable me to get rid of the nods in my thoughts, of these bulges around my stomach and it will contribute to "pushing my limits" as we say. The scholars say that in order to transform a harmless act into a routine, a habit, you have to do it for 21 days in a row... In order not to be bored, I will diversify the activities from Monday to Friday. I have DVDs of Taebo, Stretching, Yoga, Pilates, Fitness... in short, I have plenty to do... My principal enemy is my laziness, so let's start the fight laziness!

• In the afternoon it's time for the prayer of 'Asr. When I am at home, I must automatically stop what I am doing as soon as I hear the call from my clock and go and pray, because I realised that if I keep going, I am tempted to do thousands of other things and might miss this prayer. However, praying this prayer on time is very important for the spiritual journey and self-fulfilment. It allows us to learn the "know-how-to-be" in the field "Knowing how to stop".

• In the afternoon, it's also the time for a snack. As a real fan of the Chrononutrition by Doctor Delabos, I pay attention to this privileged moment. This new science studied the way our biological rhythm uses the food we eat throughout the day. Thanks to it, I learned that, depending on the time at which we eat, food intake is assimilated differently. Depending on the time at which we eat the same quantity of food, our body will benefit more or less from it, in terms of quality as well as quantity! I know for instance that if I don't follow my biorhythm, I will tend to put on weight, to feel drowsy during the day or, on the contrary, to sleep unwell at night. I will then keep taking care of my food routines, those which benefit me and I will fight against my bad reflexes.

• At the end of the afternoon, before the evening rush, I need to think about the calls that I need to make, without spending ages on the phone. I also set a limit for my usage of the internet.

To be completed...

ROUTINE:

ng routines are the most important:

- I eat something light in order to sleep well and I brush my teeth.
- I quickly mop the kitchen and the living room.
- I make sure that I haven't left anything where it shouldn't be. I close the shutters and check the counters, the power switches, the door...
- I put my pyjamas on.
- I fold and put the clothes I wore today back in the wardrobe if they're clean.
- I check the hall, the shoes.
- I pray and make the invocation which links the hearts.
- Sleep before midnight is more restorative. I forbid myself from sleeping after midnight.
- I prepare my programme for the day after. I read again the 101 things which I dream to do before I die.
- I work in my notebook and do an assessment of my day. What matters to me, isn't to be better than my neighbour, but to be better than the person I was yesterday...
- I recite Surah Al Mulk in my Isha prayer with the intention of being protected from the punishment of the grave thanks to it.

To be completed...

The simple fact of committing myself to set up these good habits allowed me today to set out my ideas and therefore, I know that I started to become someone who lives a clearer life. Our present consists of thousands of moments, while still being a unique moment, it is the only time which we can't escape. As we can't flee neither the Present, nor the here and then, why not welcome it rather than escaping it? From now on, let's do our best, that's what God is expecting from us. Let's respect Him, may He be Exalted, by escaping mediocrity and by assuming our responsibilities in the present.

Taking responsibility of every single moment enables us to have a disciplined life, ruled and oriented towards a goal: love God and have the love of God.

In fact, when we focus on our functions, our acts, our thoughts, our words in the Present, we are more vigilant and we tend to be fairer and more pious. As soon as we enter the Present with our focus we realise that life is sacred. God removed speech from me so I can work on "my roles". All the roles I've been created for, all those which I have sometimes neglected.

In fact, I am a human being and I have been created as a human being, this is the first function I have on this Earth. Even if we are all, if we accept it, spiritual beings, we are all going through a human experience, which is something which I need to accept and not deny.

"O mankind! *If you are in doubt about the Resurrection, then verily! We have created you from dust, then from a Nutfah (mixed drops of male and female sexual discharge i.e. offspring of Adam), then from a clot, then from a little lump of flesh" (Surah 22, verse 5).*

God reminds me my humanity, my origin to call me back to humility. The progressive and gradual divine creation of the human being is an excellent reminder. It makes me wonder about my initial state as a human being (defaults, qualities, abilities, limits, needs, desires...) and about my possible improvement on all levels through a gradual progress on the path as God tells us, step by step, towards the best version of ourselves. A temporal and human reality for and towards a spiritual and eternal ideal...

"Their Messengers said to them: "We are no more than human beings like you, but Allah bestows His Grace to whom He wills of His slaves. It is not ours to bring you an authority (proof) except by the Permission of Allah. **And in Allah let the believers put their trust."** *(Surah 14, verse 11)*

"So eat and drink and be glad,
And if you see any human being, say:
"Verily! I have vowed a fast unto the Most Gracious,
so I shall not speak to any human being this day.""
Quran, Surah 19 Maryam, verse 26

Confucius used to say that if we force ourselves to be entirely human, there won't be any harm anymore. This reminds me the story of a man who spoke to his friend in this fashion: "How could a God let such things happen?" His friend who experienced the same Nazi period replied: "The reason for it isn't the absence of God, but rather the absence of the human being..." My first role on Earth consists in reconnecting with my humanity, to accept it in order to go from what I am and reach the ideal of this humanity. "Ô man, you are part of the human nature, pay attention to yourself and know yourself." As Moses commanded us in the Deuteronomy. Because, as the Imam Ali said, may God have mercy on him: "Whoever knows himself knows God."

We are called Human Beings (*Insan*) only because of our forgetfulness (*Nisiyaan*) and our heart is called *Qalb* only because it changes quickly (*Yataqallab*). Reconnecting ourselves with our humanity is remembering and making this effort of memory. Moving towards excellence means preventing our hearts from twirling. And the Quran is *"...a warning* ***to mankind".*** *(Surah 74 Al Muddathir, verse 36)*

In addition to **having the heart and the mind of a resistant,** I also understood that the essential resource to use on my path will be **benevolence to myself.** "I am a human being" and as such, I have rights and duties, but I also have limits and defaults. And I must allocate time in my schedule for them, because while focusing on myself with **benevolence and justice in order to reach excellence,** I will be able to sincerely observe the moments when I will obey as well as those when I will fail. Accepting oneself with benevolence and justice slowly leads to **self-esteem**, a necessary element to our balance in this life.

In my corridor, I have hung a picture to the wall, which I really like because it reminds us of the basic duties of the human being. It was a gift by an Egyptian friend of mine. You can read the calligraphy of the extracts of the articles 1, 10 and 11 of ***The Cairo Declaration on Human Rights in Islam,*** adopted on the 5th of August 1990: *"**All human beings form one family** whose **members are united by their subordination to Allah** and **descent from Adam**. All men are **equal in terms of basic human dignity and basic obligations and responsibilities,** without any* *discrimination on the basis of race, colour, language, belief, sex, religion, political affiliation, social status or other considerations. The true religion is the guarantee for enhancing such dignity along the path to human integrity. All human beings are Allah's subjects, and the most loved by Him are those who are most beneficial to His subjects, and no one has superiority over another except on the basis of piety and good deeds. Islam is the religion of true unspoiled nature. It is prohibited to exercise any form of pressure on man or to exploit his poverty or ignorance in order to force him to change his religion to another religion or to atheism. Human beings are born free, and no one has the right to enslave, humiliate, oppress or exploit them, and there can be no subjugation but to Allah the Almighty.*

As human beings, we have fundamental rights. Be benevolent towards my humanity, it is also ensuring that my rights and those of others *"inherent to the person, inalienable and sacred"* **are respected.** As human beings, we also have duties. Made out of **flesh and bones,** I will also have to respect this deposit, take care of it while getting to know better **the soul** which lives in this body.

Dumb on the field of my resources...

Talents, capacities, potential, strengths, advantages, faculties, know-how... As human beings we all have within us multiple divine resources. Life consists in identifying them and developing these fertile lands, those of our resources, always richer than what we would imagine... After having spent my Thursday thinking about my morning, noon, afternoon and evening routines which I will implement in my life, I decided to travel on this Friday to the territory of my resources. Because it is only by drawing from them and fully trusting God that I will manage to implement these new resolutions, and maybe, I will have a voice again. I will therefore write, using my Notebook:

1 - The more I will use my capacities, the more they will develop:

I need to find and use my capacities in order to improve the image I have about myself and ensure multiple victories over my ego. Therefore, I need to identify my resources, then I will work on how to efficiently implement them.

2 – Identifying my resources: skills and know-how

Even if Islam and our spirituality require from us to be humble and modest, we have to go through the knowledge of the positive elements which characterise and constitute us on the path to self-fulfilment: these physical, moral qualities, intellectual capacities, talents, know-how, gifts, particular competences... identify them shows the benevolence and justice we have towards ourselves. This is part of faith and *Hamd*, recognising the blessings of God on us.

These resources are like wells from which we will have to draw each time we face difficulties. They are mines of blessings which help us attain our ideal. However, these sources aren't never-ending, they shouldn't be taken for granted and it is upon us to nourish and enrich them, which shows how important it is to know and define them. And know that by having an open mind, you will always be to acquire more of them...

These sources will have to be protected from the enemies of our success, against our outside enemies, those who underestimate us and belittle us... But also against the enemies within ourselves, which are pride and vanity, which makes us boast. Therefore, Og Mandino, a specialist in self-development advises us to put our hands in a bucket of cold water each time we would be tempted to boast. Then he asks us to see whether we managed to dig a hole in water. If not, then he tells us that this exactly shows how important we are... *No comment!*

In fact, the diagnosis isn't the prognosis; it's not because God granted me with some blessings that I will reach my goals. These blessings are only tools. If I have tools in my garage to turn the soil over, but I don't use it, my field will be a waste ground.

These blessings of God are only meaningful in the use we make of it. And I would go even further, I think we have a responsibility towards these blessings which God granted us from the beginning and that we will be accountable for them. "So, you had the following blessings, what use did you make of it?"

I decided to draw on my notebook my positive resources by drawi
Aren't we human beings in process?

I drew on this wall as many bricks as years I have lived on Earth, so 33. On each brick, I wrote a word, a quality, a strength, an advantage, an expression which characterises me, identifies me and makes the person I am today, thanks to God.

Active | Loving | Fanciful

Daring | Caring | Warm | Cooperative | Diplomat

Conscientious | Natural | Creative | Adventurous | Coherent

Optimistic | Lenient | Enthusiastic | Hard worker | Adaptable

Intuitive | Helpful | Sincere | Respectful | Spontaneous

Tolerant | Devoted | Determined | Frank | Reassuring

Open | Sensible | Athletic | Thoughtful | Cheerful

Then I drew the bricks that I would like to acquire, those which will come with the help of God in order to replace the bricks on the wall of my weaknesses...

Because we can't leave a wall with holes in it. For the moment, the bricks which I would like to acquire in order to progress towards the ideal version of myself are the following:

Organised

Considerate | Resourceful | Diligent | Autonomous | Careful

Finally, I drew the walls of my weaknesses, and like for the all of my strengths, there are as many bricks as years spent on Earth.

A Hebrew tale narrates the following story: *In the famous little village of Chelm lived two neighbours, Haïm and Yankel, two simple and modest souls who hadn't been granted great intelligence. While they were in the public baths where they used to go, Haïm told his friend about his worries by asking him: "If I take off my clothes, how will I be able to recognise myself after the bath?" Yankel smiled and said: "This is a good question. But wait, I think I have an idea. Take a red thread and tie it around your big toe on your right foot. So when you will come out, you will know for sure that it is you, Haïm with the red thread!" "This is an amazing idea!" said Haïm with enthusiasm, enthralled. "You are really amazing:"Of course, the thread around Haïm's toe went loose. It ended up around Yankel's toe. When Haïm was putting on his clothes, he looked at his toe, then looked at Yankel who was coming towards him with the red thread around his toe! Haïm, stunned turned to his friend and told him: "You, I know who you are... but me, who am I then."*

"Who am I?" Here is a simple but essential question. It is the only question in the world which no one else but me can answer. The answer is of critical importance and the solution won't come from examining my passport or having a look in the mirror. I will have to dig deeper to find the foundations of the walls... **Asking yourself "Who am I" gives you the clear-sightedness and impulse to become who you really are.**

BACK TO THE ESSENTIAL BEING

• Underline the passages which struck you and copy them in your notebook while saying what touched you.

• Inspiring yourself from the previous chapter, draw a tree.

• Establish your morning, noon, afternoon and evening routines in your notebook.

• Draw the wall of your strengths on a paper.

• Draw the bricks which you would like to acquire.

• Draw the wall of your weaknesses.

• In your notebook, make sure that you have answered all the questions about your good and bad habits in terms of "know-how-to"...

• Establish your spiritual programme by writing it down if you haven't done it yet.

• Still in your notebook, keep writing in the section: "My health and what I can say about it".

• Keep writing the list: "My doubts and questionings".

• Keep writing the list: "The 101 things that I dream of doing before dying".

Bonus...

• Start thinking about the first role that we play on Earth: being a human being. What are my roles as such? What are my duties? My rights?

"The human being will firstly be what he planned to be"
Jean-Paul Sartre

The first purpose of **human experiences** is to draw the lessons necessary to the **knowledge of the self and its evolution.** Throughout my life, I have experienced many things, positive or negative, which allowed me to understand better who I am, what I do and how I do it. Learning to know yourself and understanding better your behaviour mode will necessarily lead to a better management of your destiny. My personal fulfilment will in fact depend on the way I will live my mourning, by using my human skills but also my abilities to perceive and react to outside events. I think I can find at least three advantages to this: a good knowledge of yourself = a good relationship with yourself, a good knowledge of the others = a good relationship with others, and especially a good knowledge of God = a good relationship with my fate and my destiny. Imam Ali, may Allah have mercy on him, used to say: *"Whosoever knows himself, knows God".*

Unconsciously or maybe consciously, we determine about ourselves what my husband would call **"a life position"**, which depends on the value we give to ourselves. This value which is positive or negative reflects the belief we have about ourselves and about our environment. It drives our life:

• When we have a + + life position, and this is what I would like to have today, with God's help, **you think that you have value and others as well.**

• When we have a + - life position, **you think you have value but others don't.**

• Then there are those who have a - + life position, I think I am still part of it, those are the ones **who think that they have no value or little value whereas others have value, thank God.**

• Finally, you have those who have a - - life position, **they think that they have no value and neither do others.**

Knowing your life position is part of knowing yourself. I know that for the moment, I am starting at - + to slowly tend towards the ideal ++ if God wills.

These life positions don't come out of the blue, if I may say so. They are linked to our education, to the words that we have too often heard or too little, while we were kids. These words, these expressions unconsciously still pilot us today. There is the child who, seeing his parents' attitude, understood that **in order to be loved, he always has to be perfect.** There is the child who assimilated that **in order to be loved, he would always have to please.** There is the child who has always been told: "Be strong and shut up." For him, in order to be loved, he had to bear and keep quiet. He will more easily dispel the expression of his feelings and will often be cold and distant. Then there is the child who understood that, in order to have attention and be loved, **will unceasingly have to make efforts in order to deserve comfort.**

Which type of child was I? I think I was a child who believed that, in order to be loved, I had to generate pride. I think I was a child who hated disappointing my parents and always had to justify myself.

And I also think I remained an adult which hates disappointing people...and who always has to justify herself. This is therefore part of the "know-how-to" that I will need to learn and I understood it since his death: "Know-how-to disappoint" and "Know-how-not to justify myself".

What are my habits, good or bad, in terms of my "know-how-to-be", in the section "Disappointing"? Do I know how to manage my behaviour, my feelings and emotions when I disappoint someone? When I disappoint someone, who is the most disappointed from us? Me or the other one? To my mind, are there reasons, which justify the fact of disappointing people? Do I allow myself to disappoint people? Am I able to identify against what and why am I actually angry when I disappoint people and why? To my mind, is it possible to disappoint someone I love without harming my faith? My physical and psychological health? My relatives? These questions cause new cramps in my stomach, I write them down on my notebook, I would really be disappointed if they flew away from there. I need to dare answering to it today.

What are my habits, good or bad, in terms of my "know-how-to-be", in the section "Justifying myself"? Do I know how to weigh my words, manage my behaviour, my feelings and my emotions when I justify myself? When I am justifying myself, who am I trying to convince? Me or the other person? To my mind, are there reasons which would actually justify the fact of not justifying myself? Do I allow myself not to justify myself? Am I able to identify against whom or what I am really angry when I justify myself? To my mind, is it possible for me to disappoint someone without feeling obliged to justify myself? Without it harming my health? My relatives? My faith?

These "know-how-to-be" are essential, I understood it since he went back to Earth. The love of a mother is the closest to divine mercy and this evening, I wish my mum was here to tuck me in, leave the smell of sleep on my pillow and that a breath of divine mercy closes my eyes. The mourning I am experiencing isn't limited to the loss of my husband, I need to grieve what I used to receive and planned to be and to do with him. I need to mourn what I had woven around me. One of the threads which was linking me to him was complicity, another was intimacy, another was connivance. Together we had woven a piece of art... and what do I have to do today with this unfinished "piece of us"?And finally, in that which we draw with our relatives on the painting of our lives, what can we do when one of the painters is gone? What can the one left do with the painting of his life? Our bodies, our hearts, our souls had slowly tamed one another.

In a reciprocal exchange and constantly entertained by brotherhood in God, we had just started to live in harmony and then, all of a sudden, it was emptiness: neither paintbrush nor colours next to him. I need to give up on the exchange we used to live together. I need to learn how to meet him on another level of my being. It is by confronting with full force to his physical absence that I will be able to meet him in an inner and spiritual space, in my heart, where I know that I will never lose him. But I need time for this, I need to engrave in me his permanent presence and accept to keep on writing my life, to draw it, not without him, but with him within me.

What could our pain create?
What do we lose when we absolutely refuse to suffer?
For better and for worse, till death parts us... weren't we told?

I feel heartbroken, I feel the tearing apart of this garment, of these threads, of these numerous invisible and visible ties which we had established and which nourished our relationship. His presence used to affectively, emotionally, intellectually and spiritually echo within me. It used to keep me warm. I am speaking, but when I speak now, I feel cold, there is no answer anymore. It might be the reason why my voice died, because I feel that I have lost my principal source of inspiration in life.

I feel like in front of a cave, where I am screaming his name, without any echo coming back to me. When he as here, our discussions used to give me value, I used to feel that he was by my side and that I had the right to live fully. I need to learn, step by step, how to breathe myself and for myself, I need to accept that I deserve to live without him and stop feeling guilty for still being alive. Like breathing, mourning, the loss are natural processes and I do understand that they have their own conditions. The only way for me to come out of the cave is to accept to get into it by answering these questions which give meaning, life-breath and warmth to life, even though for now, I feel like I am in apnea and that my heart is suffering an open wound:

Who have I lost?
What have I lost?
Where am I at since I have lost what I have lost?
Where to find that which I have lost?
How to keep a bond with what I have lost, which was made out of flesh and life?

The pain due to a loss must be overcome if we want to soothe it one day and we only overcome it by recognising, validating and expressing all these emotions, all these feelings without any taboo or false pretence. That's what I understood thanks to God, and that's wat I try to do especially by writing. My relief is at the tip of my pen but also at the tip of what I fear the most: "suffering". Because of

fear, we don't allow ourselves to suffer. In this modern society of the im
and the urgent, we are asked to get rid of our pain quickly, but often too
We suffer from an allergy to pain, an even worse, we don't like showing it, experiencing it, not even saying it. The smallest headache needs to be instantly eliminated. We aren't taught anymore how to endure, neither how to bear, nor how to listen to ourselves. Going away from your initial comfort is regarded as an aberration in the medical world. The problem is that we often eliminate the symptom, the signal, we don't let it express itself, while it is usually there to show us the origin of the pain. In every path in life, the "know-how-to-be", in the section "Knowing how to bear "? is crucial.

What are my habits, good or bad, in terms of my "know-how-to-be", in the section "Knowing how to bear"? I need to learn how to decode what I am experiencing, feeling, bearing before wanting to sedate or eliminate it. I need to recognize and express what I think is for me bearable, acceptable, forgivable, excusable, tolerable... or the opposite; because all of this is crucial in life.

Don't imitate those which don't take the time to be "humanised" by their pains, those who, when disappointed after a break up, want to do anything to forget it and end up hardening their hearts... Live the present and calmly, the emptiness of the wait and from darkness will then emerge."

Jean Monborquette

To accept my trial and to get rid of this life starts by progressively and gradually eliminating the darkness, any trace of resentment, of anger, of bitterness and frustration about my destiny. And this is only possible if and only if I take the necessary time to listen to what my heart and my destiny want to tell me.

His presence contributed to building me, to me becoming the person I am, to give me a role in this society: that of the spouse. Today, I feel like I am cut from a part of myself, as if I had been amputated from a part of my identity. I need to live in another register, play a different role, without any script, the role of a wise widow. A role which I haven't been taught at my age... I realise that with my husband's death, that God is calling me to almost experience the bereavement of my own existence, or at least, the bereavement of my certainties, the bereavement of my attachment, of my dreams, of my projections to build new ones! Other "Know-how-to-be", other "Know-how-to-do". The "Know-how-to-do the bereavement of Us" in order to reclaim a new "I".

This "Us" which I had to delete from the mailbox to replace it by "I am not here, but you can leave a message". This "Us" which I had to put aside when I took away his coat hanging on the coat hook in the hall. This "Us" which I am always reminded of when people call me Mrs B.

I feel deep within me the need to turn my intention back to God The Immortal. I often read the 99 attributes of God, this calms me down and appeases me. He is The One Who Is infinitely present, without any risk of abandonment, break, sleep or injustice... He Is The Only One Who can guarantee me that. He Is The Living, The Unchanging, The Self Existing One. He embodies with excellence the qualities of affection, love, goodwill, compassion and mercy, He Is The One Who multiplies the rewards, brings peace and security, He Is The One Who knows what the hearts hide, Who calls to patience. **It is Him that I need the most to eternally feel protected and loved.** My husband has returned to The Eternal. This is a guarantee that, the closer I get to God, the less I will feel lonely and far away from him. This also is a guarantee to me that I will never ever lose him again, he is waiting for me there, in sha Allah, in peace.

His death has showed me how, unconsciously, I was tied to this life, not to the materialistic comfort, but I was tied to life, without even noticing it. His leaving has been a shock, a real shock because I had never experienced the death of a relative before. It's as if his leaving had reminded me of mine.

He has reminded me that we don't only die from being old or ill, and that at any time we can take off this earth. His departure is actually a divine invitation to set myself free from my immediate, ephemeral and earthly interests.

But how can we love the Hereafter? How are the people who haven't lost a soul mate supposed to desire to go there? Who and what should we long to meet? Here are some questions that we don't ask ourselves enough. People give us reasons not to love this life, but do we make efforts to open our heart to eternity, are we educated to love the Hereafter. Death, as it is explained to us nowadays scares us. The fact that my husband has been catapulted to the Hereafter, because this is how I experienced it, has completely changed my mind, changed the course of my life. I don't navigate straight anymore. I navigate in circles towards the Hereafter, towards Allah Subhanahu wa taala (glory be to God, free of any default, The Most-High, Who Is above everything).

My heart needs to get used to it, but at the moment it is anxious. A feeling of insecurity due to the precariousness of life has always inhabited me. I think I am still in a state of shock, the absence of predictability of my husband's death has showed me the raw and naked reality of life, without any concession, it was brutally imposed on me. **Can we spiritually prepare ourselves for it? Can we really prepare ourselves for it?** Some more questions which I would like to develop. At the beginning of the sorrow the family, relatives, community are extremely involves, but times goes by, the weeks, moths... everyone goes back to their daily lives.

The letters of support, the phone calls become rare. Our pain slowly loses its public side. And death is not the only difficulty in life anymore, other calamities befall us, always to remind us that life has nothing good or nothing charming for the believer.

I want to sleep, to fall asleep in order to anaesthetise and freeze the pain in me, but I shouldn't do this. The healing will take longer and be more difficult if I neglect it today. That which used to please me yesterday doesn't have any effect on me anymore. This chocolate which I loved to nibble doesn't have the same taste in my mouth anymore. I have lost the will to live, to eat, to be delighted... However, I need to enjoy my part of what Allah has written for me in my destiny... At the moment, the heart is not there anymore, but it's natural, because the process isn't finished yet. All my senses are still in bereavement. They need time to be able to allow themselves to enjoy life again. The reconstruction phase which I am currently going through is here to make me accept that the world didn't stop its crazy race because I have lost the person I loved the most on earth. In order to make me accept that I need to redefine my place in this crazy race, redefine how I want to live it and run it. The imposed redefinition of my relationship with my spouse irremediably goes through a redefinition of my relationship to time, a reworking of my routines and my habits. His loss tested my certitudes, everything I had believed about time, about life, about death, everything I thought I knew about myself. This loss invites me to redefine my own self and my values...

When I will realise that I am not fighting anymore within myself against the death of my husband, that I am not trying to protect myself from this reality, my bereavement will then be over. I will have been able then to write my own loss in the story of my life. But for now, it's not done yet. I am rebuilding myself taking little steps at a steady pace. Everything my education had transmitted to me became obsolete and useless in the circumstance of the death of my husband. We are taught how to win, build, accumulate, but are we taught how to lose? How to inherit? How to transmit? How to keep the bond with those we have lost?

I speak to him loudly and in my heart, I give him gifts in my prayers. I send him fasts, I dedicate to him my reading of the Quran, I transmit him acts of charity. I miss him so much, I feel so much pain, I am so sad. I am so proud of having been his wife. I wake up at night to pray and to tell him that I am thinking of him. I ask him about his opinion and I imagine his answers. I read his letter again, his works, his poems. I tell him that I am going to manage it and that he will be proud of me when we will meet again there. I love putting on his perfume when I go to bed and kissing his photo next to my pillow. When it's cold outside, I think about him and wonder whether he is cold, then I remember that he is there, in this hot country, far away from me... He left books for me in which he used to underline key passages. He also used to record himself on cassettes... Like a searcher, he would record his reflections and discoveries, his ideas, his thoughts. I have the feeling that he has left for me through this written and audio heritage hints, wisdoms for me to succeed.

Like a field archaeologist I look for codes, prescriptions, almost cryptograms... I also sorted out some photos, movies, memories... I have relived the best as well the worst.

"You are not responsible for what has been done to you when you were a helpless child. But you are now responsible for overcoming these experiences."

Susan Forward

Sometimes, for a few minutes, I don't think about it anymore, but I feel discomfort deep within me. And I wonder "What's happening to me? What's wrong with me?" And then I remember how and why I got to this point. It is hard to wake up in the morning with a burning heart... What do I miss the most? These carefree moments which I enjoyed, forgetting that everything could suddenly stop...

I spoke about it from the beginning with a friend of mine who divorced for the second time, a year ago. She could relate to my pain, my bereavement and the evolution of my feelings. She told me that she also finally ended up understanding everything after her divorces. She says that she understood that live means **loving in order to be yourself, sometimes it also means losing to be yourself, it's learning how to grow to be yourself, rebuild yourself, find yourself again and finding God again by being yourself.** She says that she has understood that no human being can escape the pain caused by losses, that these losses have a meaning in our existence and that we need to find it.

"Be patient towards that which hasn't found an answer yet in your heart, and you will surprisingly realise that you are living these answers." says the poet.

What meaning shall I give in my life to the death of my husband? Which answers am I already experiencing? May God grant me the patience and the foresight needed to bear what I am living.

Her first divorce made her feel abandoned, a feeling which she had already had in her childhood, but she didn't take it into account. The lesson happened again and this time, she eventually reopened the dialogue with the broken child that she had been... That's how divine pedagogy works, God gives us the opportunity to understand until we die. .. We just need to pay more attention to the messages from our destiny. In fact, her second divorce made her face this old truth and awoke a feeling of insecurity linked to her present, but also to her past. She understood that she had to speak to her parents... in order to liberate herself from their harmful influence, from their inheritance of complexes and guilt feelings, in order to definitely come out of this inherited duty to fail that they had taught her!

She grew up in a family in which she thought that in order to be loved, she had to save, help, rescue... Her mum unconsciously forced her to take care of her father in his failures and defaults. As an adolescent, period when she was expecting from her dad to give her self confidence, she had been forced to take care of her infantile and irresponsible father. Subservient as a child, by the never ending desires of her mum and dad, she grew up heavy with the burden of the responsibilities which her parents should have fulfilled. Deprived of childhood, she had been forced to grow up quick and too fast.

On top of her responsibilities in the household and in her education which would have been enough to burden any child, my friend also had to take care of her mother's psychological and emotional problems for a long time. She had carried and supported this for a while, without mentioning it! Her body, through the language of repetitive lumbagos and kidney problems was constantly howling until she freed herself from these destructive interactions. After that, she never ever had back pains. She had unconsciously developed what is called a codependent and permissive personality. In other words, she only found meaning to her life when rescuing or mollycoddling dependent and endangered souls. She grew up while losing sight of her own existence.

Whatever you don't return to the sender, you transfer it...

My friend grew up apart from her own self, apart from her life by bearing her parents, her husbands but also her friends. While trying to rescue her parents, her husbands and friends, she became herself a victim. Attracted by social cases, she had thought that by succeeding in being good enough, generous, helpful and lenient, she would manage to make these beloved people realise their failures and mistakes, towards themselves and towards her...

The first emotional relationship that my friend had with a man was with her dad. She grew up disturbed by the need of her father for her but also by the guilt that she felt when she wouldn't manage to meet his expectations. She never stopped her efforts to try and make up for her inability to make him happy, even when he wasn't there. Her choices, in terms of men, had therefore been guided by the need to appease her guilt and by choosing paternal substitutes she unconsciously perpetuated the emotional privations that she had experienced as a child.

Firstly an invisible child, she then became an invisible spouse, an invisible friend, an invisible woman. **In fact, in order for a child to formulate the meaning of value, his parents need to take into account his needs and feelings.** Her story is sadly not an isolated case, many children have been raised by parents who rob their childhood.

These type of parents focus their energy on their own physical and psychological survival and send the following message to their children: "Your feelings are secondary, I am the only one who is important, the only one in real need."

She thought that, by valuing others she would fill her need for love, for acknowledgment, her lack of self esteem. She thought she could influence these men, even her dad, and get them to understand her and love her. But these men in water, that she tried to save, never really loved her and never ever gave her anything in return, or at least, not what she was expecting. You can't save someone who doesn't want to be saved, she told me one day. That's what she had understood. Even your own parents.

Generous towards everyone but herself, she had ended up forgetting herself, and while forgetting herself, she had ended up forgetting God in her despise for men. Raised by a father -- (neither I nor people have value) and a mother -+ (I don't have any value, but others do), she had built a marital life -+ through her choices of husbands. She went through a -- phase, where even God had lost value to her eyes. But she rebuilt herself thanks to God and has understood the right order. She has understood that she had to be fair towards herself in order to be fair towards others.

She had to go through two divorces and a depression to understand this. Until she liberated herself.

These two divorces allowed her to understand that she needed to break the cycle of repetitions and that she didn't have to carry responsibilities which weren't hers. Life is made of attachment, renunciation, revelation and new start... and so on. Lessons keep repeating themselves until we grow up, until we are mature, until we dare to say ourselves, until we have the courage to be our own selves... Her divorces made her sort out that which was buried with her parents... She tried to turn her losses into the seeds for a new life, which she will nurture and grow today.

"You can still behave as if you were a child or as if you were helpless because you are waiting for your parents to allow you to be an adult. But the authorisation only comes from you, not from them..."
Susan Forward

What does the death of my husband push me to deal with in my past life for my future life? What does the death of my husband push me to become? To get for tomorrow? What does the death of my husband push me to set myself free from?

I feel like I have been catapulted on the path of independence while my whole being was dependent. I feel like I have been propelled to the apex of autonomy without having been prepared to it. I was dependent on my parents, on the well-being of my brothers and sisters and then on my husband, and I enjoyed it. But this past dependence doesn't help me anymore. On the contrary, it is an impediment and the source of all my anxieties, of my worries.

I also want, like my friend, to catch in this trial the opportunity to become more mature, to have a broader perspective of my fate and to understand all its divine messages. I would like to rebuild myself on the right foundations. I want to liberate myself and to say that which I never managed to say, to eventually be in harmony with myself. I want to say "I love you" to the people I love. And to say to those who have hurt me, the pain I have felt, the effect it has today and tell them what I expect from them tomorrow.

I just want to tell them without expecting anything from their answer, just in order to sort myself out and give myself the authorisation to grow. I want to "dare to say to people this is my true self".

What are my habits, good or bad, in terms of my "know-how-to-be", in the section "Saying yourself"? Do I know how to weigh my words, manage my behaviour, my feelings, my emotions when I dare to say myself? When I dare to say myself, for who do I dare: for me or for the other? Are there reasons for me not to dare "to say yourself"? Do I allow myself to say myself? Am I able to identify who and what I am afraid of when I don't dare to say myself? To my mind is it possible to dare to say myself without feeling obliged to justify myself? Without affecting my health? Without affecting my relatives? Without affecting my faith?

What are my habits, good or bad, in terms of my "know-how-to-be", in the section "Having the courage of being yourself"? Do I know how to respectfully be myself? Do I know how to be myself with my parents? With my siblings? With my family? What do I feel when I have the courage to be myself? To my mind are there reasons which would justify not having the courage to be myself? Who am I when I am not myself? Do I allow myself to be myself? Am I able to identify who and what I am scared of when I don't have the courage to be myself? To my mind, is it possible to have the courage to be myself without feeling obliged to justify myself? Without affecting my health?

Without affecting my relatives? Without affecting my faith? And how to have the courage to be myself? Where can I draw this strength?

At the moment, I need to draw strength from resting, my eyes are closing as I am writing these questions...

"And keep your dreams (...) you never know at what point you will need them."

Carlos Ruiz Zafon

Last night I had a dream! I dreamt of a ++ life position! I dreamt that I was doing a test and that it was ++. I woke up overwhelmed. It has been three months that my cycle hasn't resumed since the death of my husband, I don't know what to think. What if the test was right? What if the dream revealed the truth? What if it was true and this delay in my menses wasn't only due to the shock in my life, to the bereavement in my soul? Oh my Gosh! Keep calm my daughter, keep calm... But if this absence of voice for three days was actually giving me good news, that which Zakaria (peace and blessings be upon him) received in his dream? What if? What if... that's it, I am feeling sick. I feel that something is moving in my belly... you are having psychosis my daughter. My head is spinning. I need to stop, I need to call mum, that's it, I need to call mum, but is my voice back? I just cried with the crying of a newborn... after three days. What a miracle, I have found the Word again!!! I feel like a newborn. Thank you God for giving me my voice back. Oh Lord, give me a bit of time before my last rattle. Time to understand, time to feel, time to be more mature... time to learn how to live and die. Ameen.

"Hello Mummy?"

"Oh my daughter, how are you? I was worried, three days long without hearing from you."

"I'm alright, I am feeling better, thank God."

"But your voice sounds strange."

"No, everything is alright, el hamdulillah. But I have to tell you something strange."

"Kheyr in sha Allah benti*"*

"Yes, I mean, I think so? Well, I had a dream, I had a dream three days ago, that I heard *"He said: "Your sign is that you shall not speak unto mankind for three nights, though having no bodily defect." Then he came out to his people from Al-Mihrâb (a praying place or a private room), he told them by signs to glorify Allâh's Praises in the morning and in the afternoon."* You know it is the verse of the Quran about Zakariya, peace be upon him. And then, after this dream, I woke up mute. Nothing, no voice at all, I didn't want to worry you, that's why I told you that I had a cold. Anyway, this lasted for three days: wednesday, thursday and friday; until this saturday morning, when I eventually managed to speak again."

*"El hamdulillah benti**. You know, the shock you have experienced leaves effects on your soul, you need to trust Allah."

"No, mum, you don't get it, wait, I'm not done. Yesterday I had a dream, I dreamt of you and you were at mine, and I saw myself taking a test, a pregnancy test and it ended up being positive ++. "

"Benti, it was a dream"

"But mum, it's been three months that I haven't had my period."
"Me too benti, you know, when your granddad died, I didn't have my period for a whole year."

"And the dreams I had, and the speechlessness, these are signs of Rabbi*, right?"

"Benti, calm down, come to our house, we will speak about this."

"No, sorry mum, I am tired and I don't want to go out. But don't tell anyone about this discussion. You're right, it's rubbish. Since he has left, my mind is cluttered. Big hug, give my *Salam* to daddy."

My mum must be right. This dream is only the hidden achievement of a trapped desire, or maybe of a fear? Who knows? I must have read something about babies, or the remembrance of this discussion with my friend about her parents and her divorces, it must have upset me. I don't know the meaning of these dreams, but nothing in my projects on Earth should change.

I shouldn't get excited and forget about my values. They are the basis on which I will learn, they give meaning and direction to my life. They are engraved on my **"business card of happiness".** In order to see things more clearly it would benefit me to redefine them like a CV which I would have to update. I remember having done this exercise with my husband. From a list of a hundred words used in neuro-linguistic programming, this famous science which cures pains with words, I had to choose my thirteen values. I picked up my notes and read that document entitled:

List of the life values which helps you find yours:

Abundance Acknowledgment Accomplishment Increase

Acquisition Help Improvement Friendship Love

Fun Animals Appearance Learning Money

Art Association Reaching Attraction Audacity

Autonomy Authority Authenticity Adventure Beauty

Volunteering Goodness Charity Contemplation

Coherence Change Charm Choice Community

Compassion Competition Trust Conception

Knowledge Cooperation Conscience Build

Contact(s) Creativity Growth God Donation

Challenge Devotion Discernment Diversity Softness

Righteousness Details Radiance Listening Education Equality

Elegance Emotion Empathy Encourage Child

Enthusiasm Equilibrium Being integrated Being present

Being linked Awakening Excellence Experimentation Explain

Essential Facilitate Bring forward Family Fantasy

Fortune Brotherhood Glory Taste Grace Guide

Joy Harmony Honesty Humanity Implication

Independance Influence Information Ingenuity

Inspiration Instruction Imagination Integrity Intimacy

Invention Games Happiness Justice Liberty Loyalty

Novelty Observation Originality Peace Parents

Passion Nationalism Perfection Pleasure Planning

Politics Punctuality Power Take care of others

Preparation Prestige Progression Quality Quest

Refinement Outreach Reaction Realisation

Recognition Regulation Romanticism Reign

Religion Reinforce Respect Achievement Richness Risk

Routine Wisdom Knowledge Science Gather strength

Feeling good Feel Security Artistic sense

Sensuality Sociability Feeling Spirituality Service

Sex Simplicity Cure Solidarity Solitude Support

Shows Speculation Sport Status Stimulation

Success Superiority Surpass Suspense Synthesize

Time Tenderness Attempt Touch Transmit

Work Triumph Union Truth Vision Trip

Here are the values I had encircled, six months ago: **Love - Improvement - Coherence - Equilibrium - Family - Happiness - Brotherhood - Simplicity - Volunteering - Sharing - Listening - Religion - Peace**

My husband had encircled the following: **God - Love - Family - Accomplishment - Justice - Respect - Encourage - Implication - Achievement - Wisdom - Excellence - Preparation -Trust**

I remember that this exercise had been very beneficial to our relationship. It enabled us to be consciously more aware of each other's values and needs. Some of our remarks and behaviours became more understandable for us. Among these values, there were preparation, implication, trust, respect, encourage... Seeing that, it allowed me to understand better why he was always after me, until I succeeded. He used to be a man of values, and even after his death, he still is through his inheritance that he left after his earthly passage!

Today, my values have changed, I don't want to circle the same words. I realise that I have changed, that I became more mature?!

God - Wisdom - Love - Learning - Harmony - Softness - Travel - Coherence - Humanity - Family - Excellence - Light - Quest

These are the values I circled. They are my new databases, they are the headquarter of my deep identity, they express and mirror my new needs. What can I notice? I noticed that I have inherited some values from my husband, that he has transmitted them to me. My first value is now God like for my husband. I notice that the values love, family and coherence changed place but remained indispensable to my well-being on earth. Improvement was replaced by learning which became vital for me. Equilibrium became harmony, Happiness became softness, brotherhood became comprised in humanity, volunteering has been replaced by travel, simplicity, sharing and listening have been replaced by wisdom, excellence and light. Peace became quest, probably the quest for meaning and peace. These values will be guides in my life, until the next step. Being in harmony with them will be fundamental for my balance. They will enlighten my path in order for me to live my bereavement without getting lost. Every evening, I will have to wonder if I have lived in line with each one of these values.

• **God:** Have I worshipped God the way He wants me to? Did I tell Him how much I love Him? Have I been worthy of this love?...

• **Wisdom:** Have I been wise today? Have I been wise enough?...

•**Love:** Have I told the people I love, that I love them? How did I prove it to them? Did I tell them how much I need their love? How much their presence is important to me?...

• **Learning:** What did I learn today? What did I understand? What did I keep track of today? What did I transmit?...

• **Harmony:** Have I been in harmony today? Have I been harmonious enough in my different functions?...

• **Softness:** Have I been soft today? Have I been soft enough with those who deserve it?...

• **Travel:** Have I satisfied my thirst for travel, evasion and creativity which inhabits me today?...

• **Coherence:** Have I been coherent today? Have I been coherent enough in my different functions?...

• **Humanity:** What have I done for humanity today? Have I been human enough in my different functions?...

• **Family:** What have I done for and with my family today? Have I fulfilled my responsibilities? Have I been myself? Have I dared to say myself?...

• **Excellence:** Have I been excellent today?...

• **Light:** What have I done for light today and against darkness? What have I done to bring down the light into my heart? The light into my house? In my family? In my neighbourhood? In my husband's grave?...

• **Quest:** Have I satisfied my thirst for knowledge, this thirst to understand what's within me today? Where am I at in my soul? Have I written down my findings?

BACK TO YOUR ESSENTIALLY HEAVENLY BEING

• Underline with a pen the passages which have struck you and write them down in your diary, explaining why they have affected you.

Inspiring yourself from the passages in the previous chapter:

• Identify your life positions (+-, -+, ++, --). Explain why and how you have built this life position and say whether you want to change it and why?

• Define which child you have been.

• Answer the following questions about "Knowing how to disappoint" and "Knowing how to justify".

• Try to answer the following questions regarding your own life: Who have I lost? What have I lost? Where am I at since I've lost it, her, him, them? Where can I look to find what I had lost? How to nurture a link with that which I have lost? Do I really need to nurture a link with that which I have lost?

• Answer the questions about "Knowing how to bear".

• Have you ever felt a loss of any kind? If it is the case, what did this loss push you to deal with in your past life for your future life? What did this loss push you to become? What did it push you to acquire for the future? What did this loss free you from?

• Answer the questions about "Knowing how to say" and "Courage of being yourself".

• Choose your 13 values and rank them by priority (see appendix on page 156)

• Realise the Road of Life (see appendix)

Bonus

• Read *Toxic Parents; Overcoming Their Hurtful Legacy and Reclaiming Your Life* by Susan Forward in collaboration with Craig Buck, a New York Times Bestseller.

The word "quest" comes from the latin root "quaesitus" which means "research, questioning".

The word "mission" comes from the latin words "missio" and "missus", which mean "sent, pushed towards".

The word "vocation" comes from the latin word "vocatus", which means "called to action".

The word "vision" comes from the latin root "visus" which means a plan "which has been seen".

Through his reflection and his experience in the quest and the meaning of life, my husband had left for me invaluable tools in order to ease the discovery of our missions, of our vocations, those for which we are individually made, those for which we have been called, **those for which we have been created.** He has left such a precious"Know-how-to-be" as his heritage that I feel the responsibility of sharing it with the whole world. An adamic, prophetic, practical and essential method nurtured by the Quran and the Sunnah and which helps people to find internal coherence and the right direction on Earth.

Who wouldn't want to find his/her way? Who wouldn't want anyone to show him/her the way? Who wouldn't want to know how to read his/her destiny, to know how to decipher the secret code of his/her "spiritual DNA"?

To understand the states in which he/she is?

Sooner or later every single one of us will be pushed in the corner to face this, whether we are looking for it or not. I have never wanted that which I am experiencing today, but life decided otherwise, because she also has as a vocation to be a convocation! Life is a convocation to meet yourself, face your abilities, your active strengths, to face God... to face your mistakes. It is a call to the Better, a call to transhumance towards Him, towards His mountain pass: that of His Closeness and His Satisfaction. During this journey, this destiny, this migration to eternity, God makes us meet shepherds, life smugglers, sentinels that He puts here and there all along our adventure in this world.

They are settled at different stages of our life timeline in order to indicate to us how to overcome the next obstacle, to show us the next star of faith, the one which will enlighten us in this worldly life. Sometimes we might pass by these strait smugglers without even noticing them, without even daring to look at them or even listen to them. Unfortunately too bogged down in our worries we don't look at the direction they are pointing at.

"Mourn the stages of your life which you have already crossed, deepen the understanding of your identity, cure your soul, protect your body. Motivate your heart and find your mission."
Sheikh Abu El Hedi

Many of them decided to write down their advice so that we can read what they had to tell us. But too busy in our lives, we forget to read their survival guide, their GPS "Guide to Position yourSelf".

Then we wonder why we end up arriving in a deadlock, in front of a path which seems to be a dead-end... I realise today that I had the opportunity of having been married to one of them. Even after his death, he still keeps showing me the road markings. Indeed when I opened one of his books from his library, *Manhaj Al Islam Fi Tazkiyat An Nafs* (The way to purify your soul according to Islam) by Doctor Anas Karzoon, I found a bookmark on which he had written a phone number and the following recommendations:

"He who has a Why can bear any How"

Nietzsche

My heart suddenly started to beat faster. Would this bookmark be part of the messages which my husband has sown here and there in the whole flat? Didn't he say in his letter: "this first letter is only the start of a great complicity between us..."? I want to take the phone and dial this number but I am afraid. Who is this Sheikh? Do these sentences come from him?

Why have I taken this book from the library? My husband had often advised me to **study my previous intentions** in order to grasp the consequences of my actions. I remember having taken this book
as a continuous movement towards the work I am doing to learn to know myself better, from what I currently am to become the ideal person I can become. This week, after having established and studied my values, I wanted to read a book which my husband had advised me which deals with the cures and attention one needs to have for his soul. And here I am, stumbling across this bookmark, with these recommendations which strike me, I even feel like they were meant for me: **Mourn the stages of my life which I have already crossed, deepen the understanding of my identity, cure my soul, protect my body. Motivate my heart and find my mission.** It is exactly what I need.

But what's the link between these recommendations and the Sheikh's number written below?

Is he a life smuggler that my husband had met? Why didn't he tell me about him while he was alive? I am too curious, I decide to call him. The phone rings three times, ring, ring ring, will he pick up the phone? "Hello?" I was so stressed about explaining him why I was calling that I swallowed down my spit. What if the call has nothing to do with the quote... "Hello?" he repeated. "Hello, who is this?". I took my courage in my hands and replied by the islamic greeting.

"Hello, Assalmu aleykum"

"Wa Aleykum assalam wa rahmatullahi wa taala wa barakatuhu wa ridwanuhu wa maghfiratuhu"

"Erm… are you Sheikh Abu El Hedi?"

"Naam, speaking!"

"Erm, actually… I am sorry to disturb you, my name is Mrs B… and you will most certainly think my call is strange but I found your contact details on a bookmark which my husband used to use, while he was alive and your phone number was written on it under some pieces of advice which really struck me. I thought that you might be the author of these lines and that you might have known my now deceased husband."

"Don't worry, you're not disturbing me at all. In fact, I knew your husband really well, may peace be upon his soul. I was sure that you would end up calling me one day… What is actually written on that bookmark?"

"Wait, please hold the line… Here is what's written on it: *"Mourn the stages of your life which you have already crossed, deepen the understanding of your identity, cure your soul, protect your body. Motivate your heart and find your mission!"* Do these pieces of advice come from you."

"These pieces of advices don't belong to me, they are dedicated to you as much as to mankind as a whole, I just remind people around me of them because they are in line with what God is expecting from us in this worldly life… How are you my sister since your spouse returned to his Creator?"

"El hamdulillah, I am slowly bouncing back, as we say. But I have had many signs proving to me that God hasn't abandoned me. My husband was… I mean, is still a wonderful man. As you might know, he died in Medina, and one month after his death I received a testamentary letter from him. He had planned to leave advice for me if he dies before me. And what advice did he leave! Fair and loving recommendations which I use as viaticum in my life… What about you, what was your relationship with him?"

"Your husband used to come and visit me from time to time, our discussions were really rich. Indeed, he had been a wonderful man, not because he had supernatural or extraordinary virtues, no. He was an amazing man because he had accepted with virtue to be a human being with his qualities and his negative sides and because he had understood an essential thing. He had understood that if he fairly accomplished his task in this world he would be sure to find a dynamic and meaning to his life. He had therefore found, step by step, the aspirations of his soul and his reason for existing.

By the end of his life, he had managed to have the feeling of being himself, he had felt the profound unity within his being and tried to lead an authentic life, which had a positive influence on his relatives and yourself, you won't deny. At the end of his lie, he was filled with a feeling of completeness which sadly contrasts the feeling of existential void which most of our contemporaries. Most of them suffer from some kind of soul fever which is the consequence of a psychological and spiritual potential which they have neglected for too many years. You can be proud of him, Masha Allah* and you will succeed if you follow his footsteps."

"You seem to know him well and it seems to me that you played a certain role in his change. You were speaking about his task in this worldly life, what do you mean by that?"

"He managed to have a dialogue with his heart, dear sister, in order to ask the real questions about the use of his time, of his strengths and his creativity. He also managed to make use of patience in spite of his doubts, his tuggings and in the alternation of fear and zeal he managed to find the reason why he had been created. Hasn't he ever told you about it?"

"He actually never told me about you, or I don't remember him doing so. He referred to the scholars and the elders so often that I didn't remember all the names. He told me many times indeed about a mission. He told me he had been created to be the witness of God's love on Earth, to be the witness to His Generosity. He told me that his mission was to help people find their reason for existing, to encourage them and to support them in their quest...

He wanted to be a mercy for the inhabitants of the Earth and work towards his own physical, psychological and spiritual growth in order to help them more in their lives as he said. He never wanted to say that which he didn't do. He wanted to develop within himself what he called emotional intelligence in order to become a good communicator and establish psychological and spiritual methods which contribute to the thriving of the human beings. Above all things, he wanted to be an agent of God on Earth and an agent of change in his community through writing and exchanging while fostering respect for individualities and charisms... There you go... This is what I remember... Speaking about him with a person who really knew him really feels good... Thank you and sorry for taking your time...You have advised me to walk on his footsteps to find my task in this world. Would you be ready to help me on this path?"

"I was actually going to suggest this. I think that you are ready, because I can see that you have already deepened your understanding of your husband's findings. Keep on this track. I will try to help you as best as I can. You will receive in the coming days a little booklet to meditate about. I need to go, I have an appointment with God, the prayer of Asr is starting soon... Start to meditate about the advice on the bookmark! Assalamu aleykum wa rahmatullah."

"Wa aleykum assalam wa rahmatullah thanks a lot... Erm, do you know my address?"

"bip, bip, bip"

"Oh no, he put the phone down."

I sat there for a long time as if I were in another dimension, completely absorbed by my interrogations about what he was going to write me. I suddenly felt that I had become too small for my couch. My husband must have given him my address, otherwise, he would have asked for it?! But I am happy that the stone "Audacious" from the wall of my life has been useful to me today in making me dare to take the phone. I think it was a good thing that I called him. I feel appeased, as if I had been reassured about the way to follow. I need to be patient, I will receive the parcel in 3 days at least. In the meantime I will read the book by Anas Karzoon and meditate about the bookmark...

"A book is a vessel for which you need to raise the anchor. A book is a treasure which you need to take out of a locked trunk. A book is a magic wand which you master if you understand its words."

Michel Bouthot (Path sprinkled with immortal thoughts)

Three days have gone by and I couldn't stop thinking about the discussion I had with Sheikh Abu El Hedi. My mail box is for me, a real treasure trunk. Since my husband's letter, I always open it with the excited heart of a child who is expecting something... Today my eyes are sparkling, there's a letter for me. I quickly run upstairs to read it on my couch. I have the same feelings, I am shivering, my hands are sweaty, my legs are shaky. I read it out loud, as if someone was speaking to me...

In the Name of God The Merciful, The Most Compassionate, The Very Compassionate,

Dear sister,

I am sending you this letter following our phone conversation. I was getting ready to get your phone call. Having known your husband well, peace be on his soul, I was sure that you would find my contact details some day. As the Chinese saying goes: "When the student is ready, the teacher appears".

I was waiting for a sign from you because it is also my responsibility and my duty to transmit the fruits of our discussions.

I met your husband through a friend and since our first meeting ties starting to take shape between our hearts. Even stronger than blood ties, these links kept getting stronger with each exchange. The rank of a person to God depends on **his/her determination, his/her interest, his/her efforts, his/her sacrifices, his/her mastering and his/her intentions,** *and this is why I love people and I loved your husband for the sake of God. Despite my provocations in order to test him, I saw loyalty and sincerity coming from your husband. He was looking for the company of the Angels, did you know that?! What I estimated the most in this boy was his unquenchable thirst for knowledge, his desire for staying informed and his generous taste for transmitting what he understood. These qualities are so rare and so important nowadays.*

You surely must have noticed that the passage to the 30s was a decisive turning point for him in realising his missions. In fact, he noticed by being around his friends who are in their 40s that few of them are satisfied with themselves.

On the contrary, most of them were speaking of remorse, of hidden dreams, of missed ideals, of their carrier which was imposed on them, of their family being far, of their lack of spirituality. He came to see me with fear in his chest, the fear of growing older and dying with regrets. Quoting Ducharme, he used to say to me: **"It is always pointless to regret since we can only regret afterwards."** *He wanted to be fair and to make himself come true for God, in order not to have regrets. He had understood that intention is the cornerstone of every achievement. He wanted to be irreproachable, he was aiming for excellence. He used to act every day convinced that his actions could change everything.*

I am 73 years old and I have been married with my beloved wife for 50 years. She went back to her Creator two years ago. I can understand that you might need support in order to know how to keep on living and feeling loved. I don't know if I am the one who actually inspired your husband for the letter that he sent you, but I remember having told him that I would have really liked my wife to leave a letter before she left. May God bless the sincere and loving influence of his soul on yours. I am happy that he has taken the time to transcribe it. The most precious time we have is the one we invest in and for our family.

In memory of your husband, I will do my best to transmit you, as I did with him, my knowledge in the realisation of the self for a regulated, disciplined and fair life directed towards an aim: **Loving Allah and making Him love us.**

When you are a teenager you already have intuitions about your life project but you need to grow up and become more mature in order to undertake it personally. When the teenager tastes too early the essence of his/her being, the revelation of his identity, everything overwhelms him/her because he/she isn't capable of bearing the meaning of his mission and his destiny. This internal turmoil and state of mind at that moment are actually only there to show the teenager that **he/she is the key element in his/her life.** *It is his/her approach of life which will give the climate to his/her life. It is his/her daily mood which will build its ambience. It is his/her life hygiene which will influence its environment.*

It is also during this time that the teenager will realise that the adult has the power of making people's life more miserable or more joyful, that he can turn himself into an instrument of torture or into a source of inspiration, that he can despise or cheer; hurt or heal... ***And you my dear sister, which teenager were you? Which project did you have?***

What was attracting you? And why? What was affecting you? How did you want to contribute to humanity? Have you reached the goals you had set for yourself? And these projects, are they really outdated?

Your husband told me a lot about his teenage years and his ideals. He explained to me how his immaturity and his impatience made him burn his wings when he wanted to fly too early and too high. He made of this passage of his life a strength and not a weakness. As an adult, he knew how to listen to his deep aspirations and his intuitions became real wisdoms. When someone lets faith and intelligence come together in his/her destiny, it is very likely that his path will be exceptional. Your husband didn't want to be Mister Nobody. He wanted to serve the world, but for that he firstly wanted to educate himself. I don't know if he has told you this story but this reflects well how he perceived his pathway: "One day, a young lady came to Gandhi to ask him to help her son stop eating sugar. Gandhi asked the child to come and visit him two weeks later.Two weeks later, the mother brought her child back.

Gandhi said to him: "Stop eating sugar my child..." Intrigued, the woman answered: "Thank you, but may I ask why you didn't tell him this on our first visit?". Gandhi replied: "Two weeks ago, I was still eating sugar". Your husband had understood that in order to be a good transmitter, he didn't have to recite; neither explain; nor demonstrate, but live by his teachings and inspire them...

God has gifted us with free will. He has granted us tools in order to use this special ability. I think he had reach a certain level of closeness to God because he knew how to use his creativity, his talents, his originality and his dreams in the free achievement of his mission for God.

He has enriched the world with his unique and essential contribution. If you want to know this serenity of the soul you will have to learn ***to identify your talents, to listen to your dreams, your creativity, your originality to serve your mission,*** *the one for which you have been created. Don't worry, the discovery of your mission will increase your self-esteem, even though you might think that it's low right now. You will learn to trust the potential that God has endowed you with.*

The older I get and the shorter my life gets, the more God grants me the gift of clairvoyance. Be assured, my sister, that every life project is part of a bigger plan.

And like your husband's, your goal will have ***broader consequences than you could ever imagine.***

I am convinced that you can achieve your goals, with the help of God, write them down in a clear way, because clarity always comes before success, it is even its prerequisite. Luck is nothing but the combination of a good preparation and the ability to know how to grasp opportunities. ***Put your goals on paper and in front of each one of them describe the preparation they require to be achieved.*** *My work with you will consist in sharing with you all the methods necessary to achievement. In fact, as Descartes used to say: "****We can't do without a method in order to set ourselves on a quest for truth****".*

"He dies slowly, He who does not travel, He who does not read" *said Pablo Neruda.*

Thank God, I had the privilege of traveling a lot in my life. I will make sure to share my different explorations, at least those which will benefit you, before you are able to fly with your own wings. I have always asked God to allow me to meet the people who are useful to my journey. And God has always made this prayer come true. I advise you to do the same.

I remember reading Marianne Williamson's book, A Return to Love: Reflections on the Principles of "A Course in Miracles", *Ch. 7, Section 3, p. 190:*
"Our deepest fear is not that we are inadequate. Our deepest fear is that we are powerful beyond measure. It is our light, not our darkness that most frightens us. We ask ourselves, Who am I to be brilliant, gorgeous, talented, and fabulous? Actually, who are you not to be? You are a child of God. Your playing small does not serve the world. There is nothing enlightened about shrinking so that other people will not feel insecure around you. We are all meant to shine, as children do. We were born to make manifest the glory of God that is within us. It is not just in some of us; it is in everyone and as we let our own light shine, we unconsciously give others permission to do the same. As we are liberated from our own fear, our presence automatically liberates others."

This passage has affected me and many more people, but emotions are only useful if they lead to thoughtful, wise and assumed.

I encourage you, dear sister, to read the biographies of important people and to subscribe to geopolitical magazines. Make sure you understand the world as it is and not how people would like to show it to you.

For instance, did you know that Nelson Mandela had to wait until 2006 to be officially not considered as a terrorist: George W. Bush signed the law which withdrew the name of the man who led the liberation of South Africa from the shameful list! His name had been on there for almost 30 years. Nelson Mandela had made fun about this himself during his visit to the head offices of the United Nations in New York in 2001 and said: "There are some people who disagree with you and label you a "terrorist", but once you have succeeded, they treat you like a Head of State (...) the notion of terrorism is subjective." Indeed, a terrorist in the eyes of some can be a hero and a soldier fighting for freedom for others. My dear sister, make sure to put things into perspective in your analyses and not to let anyone manipulate you. It is part of the pathway to fight along the poor, the deprived and the oppressed.

As per the African saying: "Grass never grows on a path walked by all", I understood it while travelling through Africa, from the North to the South, from the East to the West. It's by getting off the beaten tracks that I made extraordinary meetings. I remember this old man in the village who used to speak to me using one proverb after the other. I made sure to write them down and they helped me to grow and meditate. Here is one of them in Wolof: "Ku xaawa de, wehku", which means "When you are a step away from death, you react".

I also remember this Zairian wisdom which says that human beings follows the cycle of a butterfly, from life to death. In their childhood they are like a little caterpillar which grows, craws until it becomes a big and mature caterpillar; then it becomes a cocoon in its old age. When the human being dies, its grave is a cocoon, then comes the command of God to tell him to fly like a butterfly. I don't know if we could really consider the cocoon as a grave, but to me the butterfly symbolises the fight that the human being needs to lead in order to carry out his mission: acquire wisdom and inner beauty. God commands us many times in His sacred book the Quran to observe nature. Dear sister, open your eyes wide... At larval stage, this animal is quite repulsive indeed. But by following the path of its destiny, it isolates itself from the external distractions in its cocoon, in order to make a whole and emerge towards the Light when the right time comes, adorned with its colourful wings.

This animal symbolises the hope of transformation. God is The Greatest! Passing through the narrow hole is the effort needed for the butterfly to be able to fly. **It is the mould through which life makes him go in order to grow and develop. Sometimes effort is exactly what we need in our lives.** *It's in Africa that I understood this.*

You will certainly find obstacles and real difficulties when exercising your missions, but you will have to hold on tight. Don't remained despaired and defeated for more than a day, pick yourself up... Once you are in harmony with your deep aspirations you will be tempted at some point to feel some pride. Don't give in, my sister, to this temptation, your work would become bland and fruitless and your good intentions will vanish and become vile. Look for your mission in humility and once you have found it, carry it out with humility like our Prophet Muhammad, peace and blessings be upon him in the Quran, Surah 49, verse 17: "They regard as favour to you (O Muhammad SAW) that they have embraced Islâm. Say: "Count not your Islâm as a favour to me. Nay, but Allah has conferred a favour upon you, that He has guided you to the Faith, if you indeed are true."

Ask God for protection from the lack of willpower and laziness. Don't lose yourself, my sister, in a state of victimisation.

Learn to identify the true nature of your wounds. Which part of you has been hurt when your husband died? Which part of you has already been hurt? Have you been hurt in your self love, in your dignity, in your self-esteem, in your pride? Has this loss awakedned a past wound? Being able to identify the nature of your wound will help you in your mourning process.

You will always have the possibility of modifying your attitude towards hardships in order to overcome them better and as long as Allah gives me life, I will help you with it. What did you learn from your mourning? Or from the offenses that you have suffered in your life? Which new resources have you found in yourself? Did you become more sensible, more human? Which new level of maturity have you reached? What have you been initiated to through this hardship? Which new reasons to live have you found? To what extent did you decide to change your relationships with others and with God?

Today, you feel a void which is normal. It's as if you, as a trapezist, had let go of the first bar and then soared towards the second one, hating the fact that it takes too long to come. You are then scared of falling, you don't know to what or to whom you can hold yourself...

And all of a sudden you see this bookmark and it plays the role of this second bar. You grab it by calling me and this was the right thing to do...

Your husband has been looking for excellence his entire life, he has tried to be fair in all the positions he has had. He has done everything to make sure that no role overtakes the other. Convinced that he didn't have much time left, he decided to live everyday fully as if it was his last day. He has written down his reflections and thoughts and entrusted you with them, because he also wanted to make a life and destiny lesson out of his death.

Within the community, he has fought with peace for wise, true and non-violent communication, against ad hominem attacks, arguments against the person. It is an evil process which sadly is very widespread among our brothers and sisters, which consists in attacking the person instead of her statement. This attitude distracts from the proposition which had initially been debated. We then pretend that the person whose opinion has been expressed is a worse human being and that's it. **Your husband always knew how to hate these acts, by continuing to love others.**

With this attitude, your husband had been the reason for many people's guidance. I liked his way of preaching, he made people want to repent. My sister, train your heart to openness, don't judge, don't be shocked, but rather invite people to go back to God.

Do it for the sake of God, do the mourning of the steps of your life which you have already been through, keep deepening the knowledge of your identity. Cure your soul, protect your body, motivate your heart and find your missions. In order to cure your soul, there is no better means than the **Quran and praying**. *To protect your body, there is no better means than* **Dhikr and ablutions**. *To motivate your heart and your spirit, read the biographies of adventurous people and of the wise and soon you will understand the guideline of your missions.*

Dear sister, implore God in these terms: "O Lord of the people, remove this pain and cure it, You are the one who cures and there is no one besides You who can cure, grant such a cure that no illness remains" (Bukhari, Muslim). The devils and their accomplice target human beings when they are weak, when they are scared, when they are angry and lose their mind.

Your husband's death has surely lowered your spiritual immune system, your gu at some point. In order to start over with a good foundation, I advise you to purify yourself, to do your invocations, to make sure to read the Quran daily, to get Zam Zam water, to surround yourself with Musk, to eat dates, honey and use black seed oil to cure yourself. Overcoming your fears and taking into account the existence of the invisible world, its good points and torments is also part of the spiritual path. The Prophet (peace and blessings be upon him) said: "No fatigue, nor disease, nor sorrow, nor sadness, nor hurt, nor distress befalls a Muslim, even if it were the prick he receives from a thorn, but that Allah expiates some of his sins for that" (Bukhari). *May God preserve you. Ameen.*

Make the Angels your allies, search for their company by making your house a place of prayer, like the mosques at the time of the Prophet (peace and blessings be upon him). Study, my sister, the house of Al Arqam Ibn Abi Al Arqam (may Allah be pleased with him). When Islam was born, the Prophet (peace and blessings be upon him) couldn't preach openly. Al Arqam ibn Abi Al Arqam, then aged 17, strategically offered his house as a place of gathering.

For three years real trainings were taking place in house. The purpose was to gather the believers to strengthen their relationship with God and purify their souls. The Muslims learnt brotherhood and love for one's fellow man, they encouraged each other towards truth and endurance. They were looking for the purity of the heart and the closeness with Allah. They acquired a broader vision of the world, combined with an understanding of inner politics. If you are able to, organise such spiritual evenings. Surround yourself with sisters with whom you can progress. Don't wait for Ramadan to make your nights moments of reverence. Never forget that every night, God descends at the last third of the night in order to answer your prayers (Bukhari, Muslim). Dear sister, seize every opportunity on Earth which guarantees that your invocations are satisfied by your Lord, before it's too late.

I preferred writing this long letter so you can have enough tools to continue that which you have already well initiated. Take action from now on and don't wait for another booklet, only God knows where I will be tomorrow. You will have to live to write and read to live a life which is worth living. Each paragraph must be appropriately meditated and applied. My sources are rich and varied like the fruits of an orchard.

Dear sister, know how to pick the fruits which you will need tomorrow from all the trees.

Fraternally, Abu El Hedi

P.S.: Back to our essential heavenly being. "Sinning is not wanting to depend from God, asserting that our destiny comes true only through our efforts, without divine help. It is pretending to be able to discern alone the good from the evil and to be able to reach salvation by yourself." Abbé Pierre

After reading this letter, I felt something unusual in my heart. It was as if Sheikh Abu El Hedi was the answer in flesh to my prayers. I couldn't help but cry. Therefore, I decided to call him to confirm the receipt of his letter. I took again that famous book mark which had been haunting my spirit for three days.

"Hello, Salam Aleykum"

"Wa Aleykum Salam wa Rahmatullahi wa Taala wa Barakatuhu waa Ridwanuhu wa Maghfeeratuhu"

"I am calling you Sheikh, firstly to thank you because God knows how your advice came at the right moment. I couldn't be happier.

By reading your letter I understood that you played a huge role in the change in my husband, I am very thankful for this and I hope you will play the same role for me. You managed to use your years of life, your trips and your experiences to acquire the keys of deep wellness and you have generously shared them. And I pray to God everyday since then to grant me life, health and faith only if it is to do the same. "

"My sister, you know, there are many things I haven't told you about and among them there is an important thing, the fact that God willed that my wife and I weren't able to have children. Even if my name is Abu El Hedi, I haven't had children, Al Hamdulillah. I mean, I haven't had physical children, but my Creator allowed me to have other types of children, spiritual children, and your husband was amongst them."

"I am sure he was very proud and pleased with this... You know, I think that God sent me the thing I needed the most since he left: creating a relationship which teaches me who I am and how to come closer to God, may He be Exalted. Indeed, I read the books which my husband has left me, but I feel that it's not enough: the divine reality is actually too intangible to be laid on paper. I also need other transmission modalities, those which are transmitted between an initiated heart and a receiving heart. God knows how much I am willing to give my heart to him. I don't have a travel companion anymore and I really miss it. It is in the company of the pious that ordinary life takes a spiritual dimension.

I found in you what I was looking for but I am afraid of having something unexpected coming up which would prevent me from getting it."

"Don't worry, as you rightly said, dear sister, the knowledge of yourself in the deepest meaning is a sign of spiritual practice. It is God Alone Who allows this knowledge and this practice. He Alone grants our organ for spiritual perception, our heart, the power to spiritually meet another heart. And it is in God only that you need to place your trust. Fear is a human feeling, even the prophets, peace be upon them, felt fear, but this fear needs to create a positive energy. Firstly to protect your organs... Because know that fear attacks the bladder, the kidneys and the bones. If you don't calm it, fear can weaken you and make you fall into depression. And when I say depression I also mean indirect aggression of your large bowel, of your lungs, of your skin and of your hair. May Allah preserve you from this!"

"Ameen"

"God created a remedy for each disease. Make sure you listen to your feelings and you find the appropriate answer to them. As I told you in my letter, I have traveled a lot, thanks to God. The fact that we didn't have kids allowed me and my wife to visit the five continents. We can say that together we have made the world tour many times... Our trips consisted in impregnating ourselves with the culture of the country we were visiting. We tried to meet all the different social classes. And we never missed the opportunity to visit universities and to stop there in order to attend some modules, when this was possible of course.

Therefore, we were able to study alternative medicine as it is applied in China, Japan, Thailand, Vietnam, Indonesia and Malaysia. It was my wife, may God have mercy on her, who was a real specialist of oriental medicine. The alliance between our prophetic medicine and the knowledge of the meridians used in acupuncture and reflexology is a benediction. For instance, when you feel some pain, ask yourself the following question: **"What does this pain prevent me from doing? What does it not prevent me from doing? What does it teach me about myself?"** This pain isn't you. It is an information sent. Chinese scholars advise us not to be one with this pain in order not to generalise it... Anyway, there are so many things I would like to pass onto you."

"...(Sigh)... How interesting, masha Allah, may God help me to know as many things as you!!!"

"He will help you in sha Allah. You will find Happiness, it is within each and everyone of us. You will only need to bring it out, within yourself, to experience this state of happiness, this state of unconditional inner tranquility, of complete satisfaction, of fulfillment and serenity. It is this state which enables the human being to say:" I am looking forward to meeting God". Most of the people think that happiness is living together as a couple, have a family, have kids, a job, being surrounded with friends, being healthy, becoming rich, having power... But these things all have a common denominator: they are not everlasting and are ephemeral; one day or the other we have to separate from them. The state of inner fulfillment is independent from our earthly condition.

And sometimes our condition can also be an obstacle. God tells us in the Quran: "Is it then he who laid the foundation of his building on piety to Allah and His Good Pleasure better, or he who laid the foundation of his building on the brink of an undetermined precipice ready to crumble down, so that it crumbled to pieces with him into the Fire of Hell. And Allah guides not the people who are the Zalimûn."

"(Sigh) ... SoubhanAllah!"

"In my letter I encouraged you to work on your objectives. But these objectives are only means to reach God. Don't focus on them, focus on what you want to reach thanks to them: serenity and closeness to God? Sincerity and God's love? Think about it!

... Pursuing your dreams and your objectives as well as the means that you will be using should never weaken your supreme aspirations in order to reap the fruits along the way. Happiness is the way... don't forget it.

If you are overtaken by the fear of not being able to reach a target that you set to yourself, this means that you're too attached to success and that you don't allow yourself failure. My dear sister, never forget that you are a limited human being and that whatever happens, Allah will never allow the rewards of the believers to be wasted. Read Surah Ali Imran in which He reminds us many times that indeed He doesn't let anyone's good go to waste, whether man or woman... Not being conscious of this shows that you don't think well of God and it is risking constantly being terrified by fear, overtaken by anger, destabilised by disappointment and being obsessed with success no matter what it takes. You will end up being attached to the results and not to God.

Results belong to God. We only expect from you, on this Earth, to do the best you can."

"I understand well, I needed to hear you say it. I promise I will make good use of your pieces of advice. I am sorry again for disturbing you. Pray for me."
"You as well, my dear sister, pray for me in order for me to do what God is expecting from me. Salam aleykum and see you soon in sha Allah."

"Wa aleykum assalam Sheikh, thanks again for everything."

I hung up the phone, softened by this discussion which brought me more than I had expected. There are first the direct and concrete teachings, then what I felt thanks to my heart. In fact, without him having to tell me, I understood that I had to accept his teachings for what they were and what they mean to me, without idealising the author too much. My husband told me one day: "Be careful, if you long for and like the company of the wise, this won't be sufficient for you. Wisdom is that which will allow you to understand, but in order to properly take action, you will first need to acquire ability. Also look for the company of the people who are skillful and handy, this will allow you to apply with virtuosity that which you will have learned with the wise, then you will have to acquire virtue because without it, you would have to settle for knowledge and know-how, without action. Be in the company of the wise, the experts, the virtuous people and you will succeed in life."

I think I have found someone who is wise, but where will I find experts? Where will I be able to be in the company of virtuous people? Those who will help me practice daily these new teachings. I put my trust in God.

BACK TO YOUR ESSENTIAL HEAVENLY BEING

• Underline with a pencil the passages which struck you and write them down in your notebook while saying precisely what you found touching and why.

In your notebook:

• Quest, mission, vocation, vision: what do these words inspire you with regards to your life path?

• Analyse the recommendations written on the bookmark in parallel with your own life.

• Study the Sheikh's letter, paragraph after paragraph. Summarise the teachings you take from it.

• Write for what reason you found this meeting with the Sheikh touching, if it did touch you?

• Answer all the questions in this chapter.

• Think about the deep aspirations which motivate your goals and your targets.

• Determine and plan the means to reach your targets.

• Taking your inspiration from this chapter, draw a butterfly.

Bonus...

Resume your spiritual programme called *wird* if you have lost focus...

"Ambition without humility is arrogance,

While humility without ambition is inertia...

Wisdom and hope nourish my actions and envies!"

I have been struck by the same incurable disease as the Palestinian poet Mahmoud Darwich: hope. And in order to cure myself I use a life long treatment: wisdom.

Following Sheikh Abu El Hedi's advice, I decided to go to the metro station Guy Moquet in the library "Resistance" that my husband used to go to, in order to increase my knowledge in history, geopolitics and philosophy. Ignoring the crowd which surrounded me on the metro, I was listening to Grand Corps Malade's song "The Heart and mind of a resistant"... Being filled with excitement, I didn't want to meet anyone, I fled useless discussions and idle and futile conversations. It was as if I was afraid that the profit I had drawn from my destiny would evaporate or get damaged before even having been able to contemplate it and seized it.

There, I filled my bag with interesting works.

My husband used to reserve every two months a budget of 100 pounds in order to stock his library with books and CDs. Therefore, I resumed this tradition:

Wasted Lives: Modernity and its Outcasts Bauman Zygmunt

Farewell to Growth Serge Latouche

Shock Doctrine Naomi Klein

The Ethnic Cleansing of Palestine Ilan Pappe

Muslim Women Speak: A Tapestry of Lives and Dreams Amani Hamdan

Where Civilisation Meet Youssef Courbage / Emmanuel Todd

Since I love comic strips, I also managed to get some nice ones there, especially *Naplouse* by the Corean writer Kim Bo-hyu.

:

Before going back home, I went to the station Couronnes in order to get some dates from Medinah, Zam Zam water, black seed oil and royal jelly to follow the cleansing treatment that Sheikh Abu El Hedi advised me to follow. My husband also used to protect himself using the prophetic medicine, he used to read Quran on water and would drink it every morning. He would do it on tepid water, because he had read somewhere that in oriental medicine, it is advised to start the day by drinking tepid water which eases intestinal transit. I will also do this from now on, read Quran on everything I buy before I eat it. I am sure this will be very good for me...

I came back home this evening, looking forward to indulge into these books. Which one am I going to start with?

"Adventure is a path with a heart."

Jeromine Pasteur Nicknamed Chaveta,
(The Butterfly of Knowledge)

After the long day I had yesterday, I slept like a baby... my head in a comic strip. This morning, after having prayed and done my spiritual program I decided to call a friend. I am dying for adventure and I know that this friend, like me, is keen on trips and expeditions in nature. Today is Monday and every Monday in the House of Mines, on Saint-Jacques' street, there are documentary film screenings which show travel stories. The globetrotters are at the event and they speak with the audience. It's really a nice concept and I will ask her to go there with me. Last year my husband and I went to their festival called "Adventure culture" and I would really like to go back there.

The adventure which had touched me and my husband the most was this world trip by the Dautais couple who traveled the world on a tandem. They had left Aix-en-Provence for a tandem tour of over a year around the world. I remember that their experience and their testimonial really inspired us in doing the same, to go explore the world on a tandem... But God had willed something different, I need to keep exploring it alone for now.

My friend accepted straight away, she even convinced the rest of her tribe. That evening, we were a group of twelve people who went to see a movie called *"The Orient on a bike"*.

Alice Goffart and Andoni Rodelgo left Belgium in June 2004 with a dream to reach the Far East using the strength of their calves. On their bike, they went through Europe, Central Asia, the Himalaya mountains, the Indian peninsula, South-East Asia, Tibet, China and reached Tokyo in August 2006. They decided to keep on their bike adventure to North America. This is the unbelievable journey of three years, three months and three days that my friend and I discovered. Alice and Andoni came in person to share their desire to discover the world in an ecological way. It was an unforgettable moment.

Since I had rested well during the day, I ceased the opportunity to invite all of my friends at home. With a cup of tea, we kept travelling and reshaping the world. This evening had been really good for me. I think again about the advice of Sheikh Abu El Hedi. I should really invite them more often, we could have theme evenings, pray together, speak about spirituality, trips, litterature, cooking, decoration... this would bring us closer and I would feel less lonely.

The moon is full and as Roland Topor said:
"You need to take advantage of the nurturing moms..."

That night, before going to sleep, my beloved mum phoned me. The discussion we had had last time had worried her.

"Hello my love?! Where were you, I tried to ring you all day and in the evening, I was worried about you."

"Don't worry mum, I just went to do some shopping in Paris and in the evening I went out with Zayna's family."

"You know, my daughter, I have been thinking about your dream... Have you had your period since our last conversation? Do you feel like you have put on weight or anything that could confirm that you're pregnant?"

"No, you know, I have lost my appetite since he left, so I haven't put on weight at all. And I haven't had my period since then, nothing yet, but as you said mum, it might be due to shock and stress."

"Listen, I actually think you should take a test..."

"You're the one who said it wasn't worth it, but if it can reassure you, I will buy one from the pharmacy tomorrow in sha Allah... It's late now mum, you need to sleep. Give my Salaam to daddy and see you tomorrow in sha Allah."

"Good night my love. Remember it's the first urine in the morning that you're supposed to use for the test, so don't sleep late. Call me tomorrow to let me know what the result is... Sorry again for calling you this late. See you tomorrow, I love you."

"You didn't disturb me mum. Love you too, see you tomorrow."

I hung up the phone with this new thought in my head. I had adventure ideas in my mind but all of a sudden she had calmed me down. Would my belly hide a little being, without me knowing it? How can I sleep without being sure of this? I took my laptop and decided to undertake some research on the net, waiting to fall asleep... I noticed that life can sometimes surprise us... I could see that there is indeed something called pregnancy denial, women who don't feel any symptoms of pregnancy, no weight gain, no sickness, nothing, but who suddenly feel pains which push them to go to A&E and there they are told that they are 7 or 8 months pregnant sometimes even that they're about to give birth... All the testimonials I read have distressed me, but there is one in particular which touched me more than the others... :

"I found out I was 7 months pregnant:

"I didn't have any symptoms of pregnancy, like most of the cases of pregnancy denial, I had my period and didn't put on weight. I could still fit in my size 8. One day at work, I was wearing a tight top and my best friend noticed that my belly button was pointing out while it was usually inside! We joked about the fact that I could be pregnant. Just for laughs, I took a test: it didn't take the usual 4 minutes to show the result; after only thirty seconds the test showed that I was pregnant.

I then decided to get a scan done to see how many months pregnant I was. Once I arrived in the lab, the doctor asked me when were my last period and said: "To my mind, one month, one month and a half maximum judging by the size of your belly." When came the time of the scan, he dropped his probe, he put his hands on my legs and said: "It's not really what I estimated at the start. You are 28 weeks pregnant... Then followed the explanation, the evidence on the scan, the tears, the laughs of astonishment, but luckily he knew what he was speaking about and really supported me. He made a referral for me with an ultrasound scan specialist for the coming week and explained to me how everything would happen and how my body would brutally change. It was the worst week of my life since I was sure that this baby couldn't be healthy: I had lifted up boxes and ran here and there at work and a week before I found out I had driven for ten hours to go skiing with my friends. Basically everything that I shouldn't have been doing, except taking drugs! So the day I was told that I was expecting a little boy, who had all his limbs and seemed in very good health, I felt reassured and managed to take advantage of the last two months of pregnancy that were left and of my little belly which was becoming rounder and rounder!!!

Two months later, weighing one and a half stone more, after a fight to get ready to welcome my little boy (documents, midwife, enrolment in nursery, new flat), I went to the hospital to give birth. My little love came to the world: 6 pounds 28, 19 inches..."

This testimonial really disturbed me, so much so that I came out of th
and went to the bathroom to examine my belly button. And you can imag
my shock when I noticed that it was pointing out more than usual, it wasn't obvious, but for me it had never been so round... Oh my God! What if I was also denying my pregnancy?! Knowing what happened to my husband, this wouldn't be impossible. Become parents with my husband was our dream... but now this is a big surprise. I need to compose myself, that's it, it's starting again... I am tired and it's playing tricks on me.

I looked at the moon through my window, the most bright parts are those which stand out the most... I want a round dream! I want God to make my belly as bright as this moon which looks like a belly... Either I moon pregnant, or I moon not... so there's no need for me to make so much drama... Come on my love, sleep, it's better for you!

To me, the best evidence of God's existence are mothers"

Children's words

I woke up with my body feeling numb. I didn't sleep well. I decided to go straight away to the pharmacy. With the test in my hands, I went back upstairs, my chest feeling tight. I drank a big glass of Zam Zam water while making a Dua to God that whatever I learn today I want it to be good for me.

The test right in front of my eyes left me speechless! They made tests now which make no doubt, it either says *pregnant* or *not pregnant*. And me, there is no doubt, in capital letters "NOT" is not showing; the word "PREGNANT" is showing alone like me in front of this test. I am pregnant!!!!!!!!!

Oh my God, I was excited, crying, I am scared, happy, a piece of him is alive within me... Oh my God! I will have to raise him alone... but I have God, my parents, my in-laws, they will help me. It is a gift from God. That's it, so I am not alone anymore. "My love, can you hear me? I am pregnant, can you hear me? You are a dad now!!!..." I am speaking to myself aloud now, I am becoming crazy. No, I am not crazy, I am just pregnant! I am sure he can hear me! I am sure he receives my calls!

All of a sudden the doorbell rang. This must be my mum, she couldn't resist...

"Yes, who is it?"

"Open, it's your mum, I went to buy you a test."

"Come up, it's open... Salam aleykum maman, come in."

"Oh my love, you've cried? What happened?"

"I took the test..."

"Ah you were faster than me hahah, so, what's the result?"

"With the new tests there's no possible error, it says pregnant or not pregnant."

"So? Don't leave me in suspense, tell me the result please, I'm going to faint..."

"Look, it's there."

"Oh my God, Youyouyouyouyouyuyouyyyyi... My daughter is pregnant, Allahu Akbar! Okay, now we need to tell your father and your in-laws, and check how many months pregnant you are. Do you have any idea?"

"No, I have no idea, but I read stories yesterday of incredible things. There are women who think they can never be pregnant and end up having a pregnancy denial. Sometimes their body doesn't change until the birth. I am wondering if I'm not experiencing the same. I am at least five months pregnant if it's the case. Can you imagine! There would only be four months left to wait."

We spent an unforgettable morning with my mum, her imagining herself as a grandmother and me as a mother. This news had been for her like a silver lining in her daughter's life, a beacon of hope!

We thought about calling my in-laws who couldn't believe what they were hearing and were so happy.

"When anxious, never lose hope, because the most exquisite marrow is in the hardest bone."

Hafiz, Persian poet of the 14th century

I took an emergency appointment with the ultrasound specialist. Someone advised me one on the Champs-Elysees because he offers to record the scan in 4D on a DVD... And many other great bonuses. The event was worth it. Seeing on a screen the fruit of the union of both our bodies moving, breathing, wriggling in my belly, I couldn't resist it, even though it wasn't cheap.

There, with my mum, the emotions were overwhelming. My dad was waiting for us in the car, he was too moved, he couldn't stop crying and me neither. My younger sister was very excited at the idea of becoming a young auntie.

Most of the mums have time to get used to their baby. They see it, scan after scan, growing up and developing. But I was suddenly going to see not a foetus, but a baby. How many months old? I had no clue, but at least five... My mum asked if she could come in with me. It hurt me when the doctor said: "Ah, the dad is going to be jealous of the grandmother..." We chose to stay quiet, we didn't want to ruin that moment. After some administrative questions, she made me lie down on a bench and basted my belly with some kind of cold gel. My heart was beating fast and my eyes were crying out of joy.

She put the probe on my belly and at that magical moment sound switched on. How amazing is that that technology serves happiness! I could hear a heart beating, She said: "Ah we can hear it well, can you hear it?"

My mum couldn't help but saying "Yes, *masha Allah*"

"Yes, I can hear it and see it. It seems quite small?"

"No, it's not very big but according to the dimensions which I am writing down now your baby seems to be 24 weeks old..."

"Which means?"

"This corresponds to a six months pregnancy. Is this your first scan?"

"Yes, I didn't know that I was pregnant."

"Ah, indeed, it happens. That's good news, you still have three months to prepare for its arrival. Congratulations, would you like to know the baby's gender?"

"No, I'd rather have the surprise."

"Really my daughter? You're brave, if I were you I would really want to know."

"Mum, I'd rather keep the surprise, for me whether it's a girl or a boy, it doesn't matter."

"Of course, my daughter, you're the mother, I can understand."

"Look, it's sucking its thumb... oh it's so cute... let's take a picture. I am saving all this so you can go back with your DVD and you can show it to the dad and to the whole family?!..."

"Thanks a lot".

I left with a sense of peace but also sad. After widowhood I will now have to learn how to live as a single mother. I am still hoping. I want to make out of these last pregnancy months strong and resting moments. Once the euphoria diminished my parents offered me to stay at theirs for the last three months. I thanked them but I preferred staying at mine. Nevertheless, they decided to send my sister every evening to bring me nice food and insisting on the fact that it wasn't for me, but for the baby. My in-laws also took things at hand, I felt like I was carried by their happiness of becoming grandparents, especially because they were missing their son a lot and they would find immense comfort with this child.

When I was about to leave, my mum hugged me tight as if she was trying to give me courage.

And then she said: "And the name, did you think about the name?"

"Mum, we still have time for that."

"Yes, you're right my daughter, sorry, we still have time, come on, go upstairs and rest."

"Salam aleykum mum, I love you"

"Salam aleykum my daughter."

Once I arrived upstairs, I felt at peace and strong. As if this little baby was already giving me the strength to fight for him. I wanted to tell the Sheikh about this good news...

"Hello? Sheikh Abu El Hedi... Assalamu aleykum..."

"Wa aleykum assalam..."

"I am calling to give you some very good news in sha Allah."

"Kheyr in sha Allah."

"Yes, I wanted to tell you that God has given me a present, a gift from heaven, I am expecting a baby Sheikh and I didn't even know until now."

"*Masha Allah! SubhanAllah... Al Hamdulillah... Allahu Akbar*, God loves you my sister. May God help you with the education of this child, but I am confident, I trust you to do a good job. The child is to the adult what the flower is to the fruit. This child undoubtedly comes from a pious lineage. Masha Allah! Don't worry, God will protect him."

"*BarakAllahu fik*, and even though I know that there are no godparents in Islam, I would still ask you to be to this child like a spiritual father."

"I gladly accept my sister, it will be a great honour for me to take care of my friend's child and this as long as God grants me life. How much time is left before his coming to the world God willing?"

"It will be in three months God willing, Sheikh."

"*Tayyib*, in the meantime preserve yourself, read about this subject, drink enough water, eat healthy and ideally organic food. Thank God and try to apply step by step the advice that your husband and I gave you."

"I have already started to Sheikh..."

"Perfect, keep doing so then and keep me updated about whatever happens. I will pray God for you and don't forget me in your prayers. Thanks for having called me, it really touched me."

"Thank you, you have been really helpful... Assalam aleykum Shiekh and see you soon."

Even if it's difficult, thank God, I feel supported. I really want to make up for the time I wasted not speaking to this little one. This evening will be our first cocooning evening together. Warm shower, herbal tea, massage with argan oil brought by my mum, Quran... a whole program. According to the testimonials, my belly will become bigger at a fast pace. In order to prevent stretch marks, I need to often apply oil on it. My friend gave me some organic shea butter so I'll alternate with both. I heard about a Muslim Mothers' association which takes care of maternity. I would really be interested in learning with them. I want to nurture my child in a natural way, by being close to my baby: breastfeeding, carrying him etc.

These mothers have a website with a forum on which we can chat, this will help me. I will contact them tomorrow in sha Allah. Tomorrow I also need to take an appointment in the women's hospital and enrol in the birth preparation courses. Since I have found out about my pregnancy at a late stage I am quite attracted by Haptonomy, which is a project which allows parents to communicate with their baby *in utero*.

The baby is able to communicate because sensory development starts early during pregnancy: all the sensory organs start working in the 5th month of pregnancy. It can perceive its environment, voices, sounds, the rocking when his mum is walking, when hands touch the belly and also its mum's feelings (happy or sad). All these sensations are then registered in its brain which is also functioning. And we also know that at the end of the pregnancy, the baby already has a story in its unconscious memory with which it will lead its life experience during and after the birth. Knowing its story, I want to give to my child all attention and emotional security that it will need to grow up and thrive in sha Allah. In spite of all the books that I have already bought, I will prioritise the book by Aviva Jill Romm: Natural Pregnancy Book: *Your Complete Guide to a Safe, Organic Pregnancy and Childbirth with Herbs, Nutrition, and Other Holistic Choices.*

I need to remember to tell my friends... I also need to prepare a room for baby... The most difficult thing will be to choose the baby's name... My mind is full of thoughts but it's making me feel good. If it was a girl, my husband and I said we would call her Madinah, but we had no ideas for a boy. My mother-in-law told me that the shape of my belly makes her think that it is a boy. I think that these things belong to God and Him only knows what the wombs contain. My younger sister bought me a Ticker, it's cute, it's a kind of dynamic and personalised calendar which counts the days left before the eagerly awaited moment.

I didn't have any cravings until I was told that I was pregnant. No sushis anymore, now everything needed to be cooked.

Thank God, my blood tests results were all fine. I spent the last two months of my pregnancy reading, walking and resting... I wanted green around me and wanted to relax... My father offered to take me to my aunt a few kilometers away from Paris. I accepted in order to be able to breathe fresher air, my belly had become really round and since the haptonomy sessions I could fully feel my baby: we had our meet ups and our codes to communicate... I went back home on the 35th week. I had to organise myself for the birth, get my suitcase ready, etc.

On top of my personal development diary, I wanted to create another one especially dedicated to the end of my pregnancy, to my sensations, my feelings, my memories... I also made an album with all the pictures of my husband so that our child can see his father's face. In his notebook, I drew the wheel of life and I wrote down my thirteen values, those that I wanted to pass onto him with faith:

To You

God: My child, never forget that, no matter what happens, God loves you...

Wisdom: I pray God that He gives you wisdom to humbly reach your goals and your aspirations.

Love: Even if I love you and you love me, we might sometimes be disappointed with each other, but this shouldn't change our feelings for each other.

Learning: We will learn together how to love each other, listen to each other, understand each other, to say each other and to get to know each other.

Harmony: We will strive to live in harmony with our environment.

Softness: I will be a soft and tender mother, my child, and I will sing soft songs so that you fall asleep while sucking your thumb...

Travel: I will share with you the love for travel and adventures.

Coherence: I will make sure I am coherent and fair and I will help you find your way, the one for which you have been sent here.

Humanity: I will share with you my love for people.

Family: We will spend time with our family and I will help you get to know your dad and be proud of him.

Excellence: I will respect your limits, your failures, your needs and will help you to go from the person you are to the ideal version of yourself.

Light: I will make a light out of your nest.

Quest: I will help you to undertake the 101 things that you would like to do before dying and I will teach you the quest for the love of the Hereafter.

FIRST CRY...

It was five in the morning on that day, the air I was breathing was lighter than usual. A thin rain of peace and serenity was falling on me from a Musk cloud hanging from the ceiling. I don't know if this is what human beings feel when they're close to Angels, but this well-being had only surrounded me once...

After having spent the night praying, I asked my sister to go and wake up my parents who live a few blocks away from me. Everything was ready, the water of life had just started to drop... My father panicking ran up the stairs and in no time the suitcase and everyone was on the way to the hospital. In order to calm me down, my father played the Quran in his car. My mum was softly repeating to me: "Breathe my daughter, breathe, say "Bismillah" and breathe, we're almost there."

Once we arrived there, thank God, the medical staff made my place ready and examined me. Labour had really started... I was thinking very hard about my husband, I could feel that from wherever he was, he was praying. I could feel him here, right next to me. It was as if someone had covered my ears with two big shells, my eyes closed, my heart started weeping. I dived, I dived... within myself 20,000 miles under the mother sea...

A few minutes later, the cry of life sounded in the room... Him and me just experienced our moment of liberating delivery.

The nurse told me: "I have never seen such an easy birth. In spite of the contractions, you looked so beautiful and look at this child how beautiful it is..." In fact, when I lifted my head towards it, there was such a bright light coming from him that we started crying and God guides towards light whomever He wills. My son was born in front of my dazzled eyes, I already loved him for life!

"Have you chosen a name Madame?

"No, not yet, but the heavenly essential is that we are beings which love each other..."

BACK TO YOUR ESSENTIAL HEAVENLY BEING

• Underline with a pencil the passages which touched you and write them down in your notebook while precising what affected you and why

In your notebook:

• Take stock of the teachings you can take from this expedition towards your Essential Heavenly Being.

• Think about the words: Ambition - Humility - Wisdom - Spirit.

• Tidy and sort out your library...

• Think about this Essential birth.

• Think about the values passed onto the child.

Bonus

• Do the exercise in the appendix called "I want to tell a tale about my birth, a touch of my childhood... At the beginning I was a seed... and my name is..."

APPENDICES

13 VALUES

This is a list of values in order to help you identify yours. Circle 13 of them.

Abundance Acceptation Accomplishment Increase

Acquisition Help Improvement Friendship Love

Amusement Animals Appearance Learning Money

Art Association Reach Attraction Audacity

Autonomy Authority Authenticity Adventure Beauty

Volunteering Goodness Beneficence Contemplation

Coherence Change Charm Choice Community

Compassion Competition Trust Conception Knowledge

Cooperation Conscience Build Contact(s) Creativity

Growth Congruence God Gift Challenge Devotion

Discernment Diversity Softness Righteousness Details

Radiance Listening Education Equality Elegance

Emotion Empathy Encourage Child Enthusiasm

Balance Being integrated Being present Being linked

Awakening Excellence Experimentation Explain

Essential Facilitate Progress Family Fantasy

Fortune Brotherhood Glory Taste Grace Guide

Joy Harmony Honesty Implication Independence

Influence Information Ingenuity Inspiration Instruction

Imagination Integrity Intimacy Invention Game

Happiness Justice Liberty Loyalty Light Home

Master Morality Music Nourish Novelty

Observation Originality Peace Parents Passion

Nationalism Perfection Pleasure Planification

Politics Punctuality Power Take care of others

Preparation Prestige Progression Quality Quest

Refinement Reaction Realisation Recognition

Regulation Romanticism Reign Religion Reinforce

Respect Richness Risk Routine Wisdom

Understanding Science Decompress Well being Feel

Security Artistic sense Sensuality Sociability Feeling

Spirituality Service Sex Simplicity Cure Solidarity

Solitude Support Shows Speculations Sports

Status Stimulation Success Superiority Surpass

Suspense Synthesize Time Tenderness Attempt

Touch Transmit Work Triumph Union Truth

Vision Trips

THE WHEEL OF LIFE

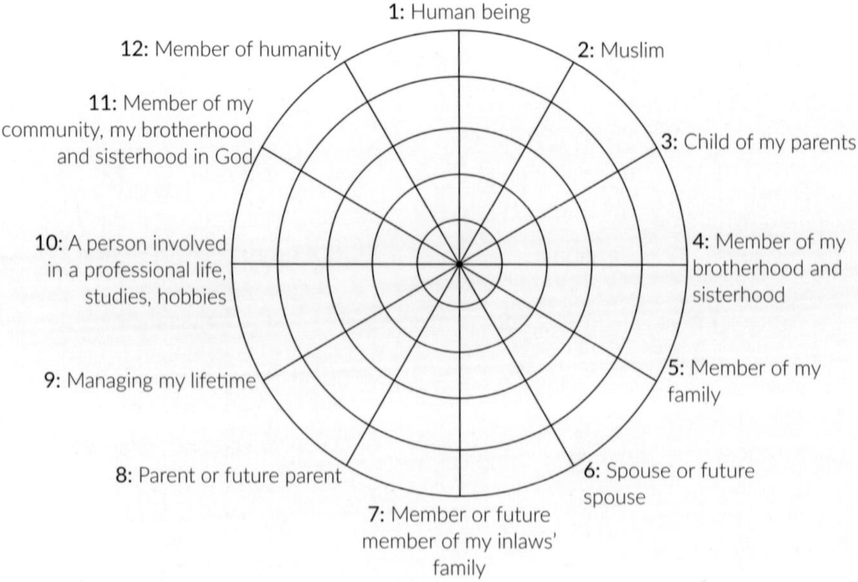

The twelve rays correspond to the essential roles and functions that we occupy on Earth. They merge at the heart of the sketch in order to make a coherent picture: a harmonious, regulated, wise, fair and disciplined life which targets a specific goal: to love God and be loved by Him.

Within the wheel of life, each of the twelve functions has five degrees of fulfillment.

It is a sketch which allows us to go from what we currently are, what we are experiencing now in order to reach our ideal: progress towards excellence on all levels.

This wheel is an excellent visual to reveal the domains of our life which show a major imbalance and which prevents things from running true in our daily lives... Sometimes the success in one field has been reached in spite of another one. Therefore, you will need to rebalance it...

The most important thing for you is not to reach perfection but to tend towards the fairest progress in all the aspects of your life.

First function that we occupy on Earth:
I am a human being

1: Human being
2: Muslim
3: Child of my parents
4: Member of my brotherhood and sisterhood
5: Member of my family
6: Spouse or future spouse
7: Member or future member of my in laws' family
8: Parent or future parent
9: Managing my lifetime
10: As a person involved in a professional life, studies, hobbies
11: Member of my community, my brotherhood and sisterhood in God
12: Member of humanity

a) Do you follow every day of your life the 13 values that you have circled?
not at all
not enough
more or less
enough
completely

b) Do you take care of yourself (physically, intellectually, health, food, life hygiene...)?
not at all
not enough
more or less
enough
completely

c) Do you respect your needs?
not at all
not enough
more or less
enough
completely

d) Do you consider yourself as a woman or a man of value?
not at all
not enough
more or less
enough
completely

e) Does that which you do for yourself correspond to what you really want?
not at all
not enough
more or less
enough
completely

Circle, add the numbers up then divided by 5. Place a dot on the sketch on page 158 to represent your result. E.g.: you have chosen the following answers: a5, b3, c1, d5, e1= 2+3+1+5+1= 15 divided by 5 = 3. On the ray "Human being" on the wheel of life, draw a dot on the 3rd circle starting from the centre. In the end, link the dots of the 12 domains together.

Second function that we occupy on Earth:
I am a Muslim(ah)

1: Human being
2: Muslim
3: Child of my parents
4: Member of my brotherhood and sisterhood
5: Member of my family
6: Spouse or future spouse
7: Member or future member of my in laws' family
8: Parent or future parent
9: Managing my lifetime
10: As a person involved in a professional life, studies, hobbies
11: Member of my community, my brotherhood and sisterhood in God
12: Member of humanity

a) How do you live your Islam?

it's very hard
it's hard
quite well
well
it is fulfilled and growing

b) Do you have a daily relationship with the Quran?

not at all
once every 3 days
once a week
twice a week
everyday

c) Do you manage to focus in your prayers?

not at all
not enough
more or less
enough
completely

d) Do you perform daily voluntary deeds (prayer, fast...)?

not at all
not enough
more or less
enough
completely

e) Do you think that what you are currently doing for your spirituality corresponds to what you really want?

not at all
not enough
more or less
enough
completely

Circle, add the numbers up then divided by 5. Place a dot on the sketch on page 154 to represent your result.

Third function that we occupy on Earth:

I am my parents' child (my parents are alive)

1: Human being
2: Muslim
3: Child of my parents
4: Member of my brotherhood and sisterhood
5: Member of my family
6: Spouse or future spouse
7: Member or future member of my in laws' family
8: Parent or future parent
9: Managing my lifetime
10: As a person involved in a professional life, studies, hobbies
11: Member of my community, my brotherhood and sisterhood in God
12: Member of humanity

a) Do you have a good relationship with your dad?

not at all
not really
more or less
yes
completely

b) Do you have a good relationship with your mum?

not at all
not really
more or less
yes
completely

c) Do you feel like your parents understand you?

not at all
partly (only one of them)
more or less (both of them)
enough
completely

d) Do you manage to show them your love, your feelings, your emotions and your questionings?

not at all
partly (only to one of them)
more or less (to both of them)
enough
completely

e) Do you think that what you are doing with and for your parents corresponds to what you really want to do?

not at all
not enough
more or less
enough
completely

Circle, add the numbers up then divided by 5. Place a dot on the sketch on page 154 to represent your result.

Third function that we occupy on Earth:

I keep being my parents' child even though my parents are deceased

1: Human being
2: Muslim
3: Child of my parents
4: Member of my brotherhood and sisterhood
5: Member of my family
6: Spouse or future spouse
7: Member or future member of my in laws' family
8: Parent or future parent
9: Managing my lifetime
10: As a person involved in a professional life, studies, hobbies
11: Member of my community, my brotherhood and sisterhood in God
12: Member of humanity

a) Do you have good memories of your relationship with your dad?

not at all
some
more or less
yes
completely

b) Do you have good memories of your relationship with your mum?

not at all
some
more or less
yes
completely

c) Do you manage to pray for them?

not at all
partly (only for one of them)
more or less (for both)
enough
completely

d) Do you feel like you have managed to overcome and accept this trial?

not at all
not really
more or less
almost
completely

e) Do you think that what you are doing for your late parents corresponds to what you really want to do?

not at all
partly (only for one of them)
more or less (for both of them)
enough
completely

Circle, add the numbers up then divided by 5. Place a dot on the sketch on page 154 to represent your result.

Fourth function that we occupy on Earth:
I am a member of my brotherhood

1: Human being
2: Muslim
3: Child of my parents
4: Member of my brotherhood and sisterhood
5: Member of my family
6: Spouse or future spouse
7: Member or future member of my in laws' family
8: Parent or future parent
9: Managing my lifetime
10: As a person involved in a professional life, studies, hobbies
11: Member of my community, my brotherhood and sisterhood in God
12: Member of humanity

a) Do you have a good relationship with your siblings?
not at all
not really
more or less
yes
completely

b) Do you spend enough time with your siblings (visiting them, calling them, showing attention to them…)?
not at all
not really
more or less
yes
completely

c) Do you feel that they understand you and listen to you?
not at all
not really
more or less
yes
completely

d) Do you take your share of responsibilities towards your siblings?
not at all
not really
more or less
yes
completely

e) Do you think that what you are doing for your siblings corresponds to what you really want to do?
not at all
not really
more or less
yes
completely

Circle, add the numbers up then divided by 5. Place a dot on the sketch on page 154 to represent your result.

Fourth function that we occupy on Earth:

I am my parents' only child

1: Human being
2: Muslim
3: Child of my parents
4: Member of my brotherhood and sisterhood
5: Member of my family
6: Spouse or future spouse
7: Member or future member of my in laws' family
8: Parent or future parent
9: Managing my lifetime
10: As a person involved in a professional life, studies, hobbies
11: Member of my community, my brotherhood and sisterhood in God
12: Member of humanity

a) Have you accepted your status as an only child?

not at all
not really
more or less
yes
completely

b) Have you suffered from loneliness?

not at all
not really
more or less
yes
completely

c) Did you feel more cherished and privileged thanks to your status of only child?

not at all
partly (by one of the parents)
more or less
yes
completely

d) Did you feel like you were suffocating?

not at all
partly (due to one of the parents)
more or less
yes
completely

e) Does this status of only child still harm you today?

on the contrary
not at all
sometimes
often
daily

Circle, add the numbers up then divided by 5. Place a dot on the sketch on page 154 to represent your result.

Fifth function that we occupy on Earth:

I am a member of my family

1: Human being
2: Muslim
3: Child of my parents
4: Member of my brotherhood and sisterhood
5: Member of my family
6: Spouse or future spouse
7: Member or future member of my in laws' family
8: Parent or future parent
9: Managing my lifetime
10: As a person involved in a professional life, studies, hobbies
11: Member of my community, my brotherhood and sisterhood in God
12: Member of humanity

a) Do you have a good relationship with your family (grandparents, uncles, aunts, cousins)?

not at all
on the contrary
partly (with some of them)
almost with everyone
completely

b) Do you spend enough time with your family (visiting them, calling them, showing attention to them...)?

not at all
only sometimes
partly
regularly
daily

c) Do you feel like your family understands you and listens to you?

not at all
on the contrary
partly (only some of them)
almost everyone
completely

d) Do you think that you are taking full responsibility within your family?

not at all
only sometimes
partly
in general
completely

e) Do you think that what you are doing for your family corresponds to what you really want?

not at all
insufficiently
more or less
enough
completely

Circle, add the numbers up then divided by 5. Place a dot on the sketch on page 154 to represent your result.

Sixth function that we occupy on Earth:

I am the spouse of

1: Human being
2: Muslim
3: Child of my parents
4: Member of my brotherhood and sisterhood
5: Member of my family
6: Spouse or future spouse
7: Member or future member of my in laws' family
8: Parent or future parent
9: Managing my lifetime
10: As a person involved in a professional life, studies, hobbies
11: Member of my community, my brotherhood and sisterhood in God
12: Member of humanity

a) Going back to your 13 values, does your spouse enable you to fulfill the values and fundamentals of your life:

not at all
on the contrary
partly
almost always
completely

b) Do you have a good communication with your spouse?

not at all
on the contrary
partly
almost always
completely

c) Do you have common dreams and projects with your spouse?

not at all
not enough
some
enough
completely

d) Do you manage to show him/her your love, your emotions, your feelings, your questionings?

not at all
partly
more or less
enough
completely

e) Do you think that what you are doing for your relationship corresponds to what you want?

not at all
not enough
more or less

Circle, add the numbers up then divided by 5. Place a dot on the sketch on page 154 to represent your result.

Sixth function that we occupy on Earth:

I am a future spouse

1: Human being
2: Muslim
3: Child of my parents
4: Member of my brotherhood and sisterhood
5: Member of my family
6: Spouse or future spouse
7: Member or future member of my in laws' family
8: Parent or future parent
9: Managing my lifetime
10: As a person involved in a professional life, studies, hobbies
11: Member of my community, my brotherhood and sisterhood in God
12: Member of humanity

a) Have you already defined the profile of your future spouse?

not at all
insufficiently
more or less
sufficiently
completely

b) Are you actively looking for a spouse?

not at all
on the contrary
more or less
sufficiently
completely

c) Do you feel ready for married life?

not at all
insufficiently
more or less
sufficiently
completely

d) Do you feel like you really know yourself?

not at all
not enough
more or less
sufficiently
completely

e) Do you think that what you are currently doing for your status of future spouse in sha Allah corresponds to what you would really want?

not at all
not enough
more or less
enough
completely

Circle, add the numbers up then divided by 5. Place a dot on the sketch on page 154 to represent your result.

Seventh function that we occupy on Earth:

I am a member of my in laws' family

1: Human being
2: Muslim
3: Child of my parents
4: Member of my brotherhood and sisterhood
5: Member of my family
6: Spouse or future spouse
7: Member or future member of my in laws' family
8: Parent or future parent
9: Managing my lifetime
10: As a person involved in a professional life, studies, hobbies
11: Member of my community, my brotherhood and sisterhood in God
12: Member of humanity

a) Do you have a good relationship with your in laws?

not at all
insufficiently
partly
almost always
completely

b) Do you spend enough time (visiting them, calling them, showing them attention) with your in laws?

not at all
too much
only now and then
regularly
sufficiently

c) Do you feel like your in laws understand you and listen to you?

not at all
on the contrary
partly (some of them)
almost always
completely

d) Do you feel like you are taking your responsibilities within your family with your in laws?

not at all
only now and then
more or less
almost
completely

e) Do you think that what you are currently doing for and with your in laws corresponds to what you would really like to do?

not at all
insufficiently
more or less
sufficiently
completely

Circle, add the numbers up then divided by 5. Place a dot on the sketch on page 154 to represent your result.

Seventh function that we occupy on Earth:
I am a future member of my in laws' family

1: Human being
2: Muslim
3: Child of my parents
4: Member of my brotherhood and sisterhood
5: Member of my family
6: Spouse or future spouse
7: Member or future member of my in laws' family
8: Parent or future parent
9: Managing my lifetime
10: As a person involved in a professional life, studies, hobbies
11: Member of my community, my brotherhood and sisterhood in God
12: Member of humanity

a) What is your opinion or the image you have about in laws?

no opinion
very bad image
it depends
positive
realistic

b) Do you think that knowing your in laws is important in making your choice for the right husband?

not at all
it depends
absolutely
it's necessary
it's crucial

c) Do you think you master the art of "How to get along with your in laws"?

not at all
I need to think about it
more or less
almost
sufficiently

d) Do you know the responsibilities of the son in law/ daughter in law?

not at all
I need to think about it
more or less
almost
sufficiently

e) Are you conscious that they will be your children's future grandparents?

yes, so what?
insufficiently
more or less
sufficiently
completely

Circle, add the numbers up then divided by 5. Place a dot on the sketch on page 154 to represent your result.

Eighth function that we occupy on Earth:

I am a parent

1: Human being
2: Muslim
3: Child of my parents
4: Member of my brotherhood and sisterhood
5: Member of my family
6: Spouse or future spouse
7: Member or future member of my in laws' family
8: Parent or future parent
9: Managing my lifetime
10: As a person involved in a professional life, studies, hobbies
11: Member of my community, my brotherhood and sisterhood in God
12: Member of humanity

a) Do you manage to pass your 13 values onto your children?

not at all
on the contrary
partly
almost
completely

b) Do you have a good communication with your children (wise, true, non-violent communication)?

not at all
on the contrary
partly
almost
completely

c) Do you share projects, dreams and hobbies with your kids?

not at all
not enough
some
sufficiently
completely

d) Do you manage to show them your love, your feelings, your emotions and questionings?

not at all
partly
more or less
sufficiently
completely

e) Do you think that what you are currently doing for your children corresponds to what you would like to do?

not at all
enough
more or less
enough
completely

Circle, add the numbers up then divided by 5. Place a dot on the sketch on page 154 to represent your result.

Eighth function that we occupy on Earth:
I am a future parent

1: Human being
2: Muslim
3: Child of my parents
4: Member of my brotherhood and sisterhood
5: Member of my family
6: Spouse or future spouse
7: Member or future member of my in laws' family
8: Parent or future parent
9: Managing my lifetime
10: As a person involved in a professional life, studies, hobbies
11: Member of my community, my brotherhood and sisterhood in God
12: Member of humanity

a) Have you defined which kind of parent you want to be?
not at all
insufficiently
more or less
sufficiently
completely

b) Are you gaining knowledge about this subject?
not at all
insufficiently
more or less
sufficiently
completely

c) Do you feel that you are ready to become a parent?
not at all
insufficiently
more or less
sufficiently
completely

d) Have you learnt lessons from your own childhood?
not at all
insufficiently
more or less
sufficiently
completely

e) Do you think that what you are currently doing for your future status of parent in sha Allah corresponds to what you really want?
not at all
insufficiently
more or less
sufficiently
completely

Circle, add the numbers up then divided by 5. Place a dot on the sketch on page 154 to represent your result.

Ninth function that we occupy on Earth:

I am Manager of my personal time

1: Human being
2: Muslim
3: Child of my parents
4: Member of my brotherhood and sisterhood
5: Member of my family
6: Spouse or future spouse
7: Member or future member of my in laws' family
8: Parent or future parent
9: Managing my lifetime
10: As a person involved in a professional life, studies, hobbies
11: Member of my community, my brotherhood and sisterhood in God
12: Member of humanity

a) Do you think that you are organised?

not at all
insufficiently
more or less
sufficiently
completely

b) Are you stressed out?

constantly
daily
sometimes
rarely
only exceptionally

c) Are you late sometimes?

constantly
daily
sometimes
rarely
only exceptionally

d) Do you think that you are giving enough time to the different functions that you occupy on Earth?

not at all
insufficiently
partly
sufficiently
completely

e) Do you think that what you are currently doing to manage your time corresponds to what you really want?

not at all
not enough
more or less
enough
completely

Circle, add the numbers up then divided by 5. Place a dot on the sketch on *page 154* *to represent your result.*

Tenth function that we occupy on Earth:
I work, I am an employee

1: Human being
2: Muslim
3: Child of my parents
4: Member of my brotherhood and sisterhood
5: Member of my family
6: Spouse or future spouse
7: Member or future member of my in laws' family
8: Parent or future parent
9: Managing my lifetime
10: As a person involved in a professional life, studies, hobbies
11: Member of my community, my brotherhood and sisterhood in God
12: Member of humanity

a) Do you feel that you are self fulfilled in your job?
not at all
insufficiently
more or less
in general
completely

b) Do you have responsibilities that you deserve to hold?
not at all
insufficiently
more or less
in general
completely

c) Does your salary match your skills?
not at all
insufficiently
more or less
in general
completely

d) Do you feel like you are communicating well with others?
not at all
insufficiently
partly
sufficiently
completely

e) Do you think that what you are currently doing as a job corresponds to what you really want?
not at all
not enough
more or less
enough
completely

Circle, add the numbers up then divided by 5. Place a dot on the sketch on page 154 to represent your result.

Tenth function that we occupy on Earth:

I am a student

1: Human being
2: Muslim
3: Child of my parents
4: Member of my brotherhood and sisterhood
5: Member of my family
6: Spouse or future spouse
7: Member or future member of my in laws' family
8: Parent or future parent
9: Managing my lifetime
10: As a person involved in a professional life, studies, hobbies
11: Member of my community, my brotherhood and sisterhood in God
12: Member of humanity

a) Do you feel that you are self-fulfilled in your studies?

not at all
insufficiently
more or less
in general
completely

b) Do you know where you are heading to in terms of career?

not at all
insufficiently
more or less
in general
completely

c) Do you think that you are fulfilling your responsibilities as a student (homework, studying, present...)?

not at all
insufficiently
more or less
in general
completely

d) Do you communicate well with others?

not at all
insufficiently
partly
sufficiently
completely

e) Do you think that what you are currently doing in your studies corresponds to what you really want to do?

not at all
not enough
more or less
enough
completely

Circle, add the numbers up then divided by 5. Place a dot on the sketch on page 154 to represent your result.

Tenth function that we occupy on Earth:

I don't study, I don't work but I have other activities and occupations

1: Human being
2: Muslim
3: Child of my parents
4: Member of my brotherhood and sisterhood
5: Member of my family
6: Spouse or future spouse
7: Member or future member of my in laws' family
8: Parent or future parent
9: Managing my lifetime
10: As a person involved in a professional life, studies, hobbies
11: Member of my community, my brotherhood and sisterhood in God
12: Member of humanity

a) Apart from the activities which are linked to the roles of being human, a Muslim, your parents' child, a member of your family, a spouse, etc., do you have any other activities?

not at all
I need to think about it
more or less
sufficiently
reasonably

b) Do you feel bored sometimes?

constantly
too often
more or less
rarely
never

c) Do you manage to thrive?

not at all
insufficiently
more or less
in general
completely

d) Do you feel lonely?

constantly
daily
sometimes
rarely
only exceptionally

e) Do you think that your occupations correspond to what you really want?

not at all
not enough
more or less
enough
completely

Circle, add the numbers up then divided by 5. Place a dot on the sketch on page 154 to represent your result.

Eleventh function that we occupy on Earth:

I am a member of my community

1: Human being
2: Muslim
3: Child of my parents
4: Member of my brotherhood and sisterhood
5: Member of my family
6: Spouse or future spouse
7: Member or future member of my in laws' family
8: Parent or future parent
9: Managing my lifetime
10: As a person involved in a professional life, studies, hobbies
11: Member of my community, my brotherhood and sisterhood in God
12: Member of humanity

a) Do you feel self-fulfilled within your community?

not at all
insufficiently
more or less
in general
completely

b) Do you think that you are spending enough time with your community?

not at all
insufficiently
more or less
in general

c) Do you think that you are taking on your responsibilities as a member of the Muslim community?

not at all
insufficiently
more or less
in general
completely

d) Do you communicate well with the other members of the community?

not at all
insufficiently
partly
in general
completely

e) Do you think that what you are currently doing within and for the community corresponds to what you really want to do?

not at all
not enough
more or less
enough
completely

Circle, add the numbers up then divided by 5. Place a dot on the sketch on page 154 to represent your result.

Twelfth function that we occupy on Earth:

I am a citizen of the world, my roles and involvements on Earth

1: Human being
2: Muslim
3: Child of my parents
4: Member of my brotherhood and sisterhood
5: Member of my family
6: Spouse or future spouse
7: Member or future member of my in laws' family
8: Parent or future parent
9: Managing my lifetime
10: As a person involved in a professional life, studies, hobbies
11: Member of my community, my brotherhood and sisterhood in God
12: Member of humanity

a) Do you relate to what is happening around you (world, district, neighbourhood…)

not at all
insufficiently
more or less
in general
completely

b) Have you thought about the positive marks that you want to leave after your passage on Earth?

not at all
insufficiently
more or less
in general
daily

c) Do you think that you are taking on your responsibility as a citizen of the world?

not at all
insufficiently
more or less
in general
completely

d) Do you communicate well with your other human brothers and sisters?

not at all
insufficiently
partly
in general
completely

e) Do you think that what you are currently doing for and within humanity corresponds to what you really want?

not at all
not enough
more or less
enough
completely

Circle, add the numbers up then divided by 5. Place a dot on the sketch on page 154 to represent your result.

AFTER THE WHEEL...

Answer these questions after having completed your wheel, they are applicable to all the functions that you occupy on Earth and of which you aren't satisfied.

What have you done up until now to improve the situation (list all the actions that you have undertaken in order to solve the problem(s) linked to the functions you occupy)?

Were these actions sufficient or appropriate to the situation?

Were you conscious of the problem?

Did you have enough willpower to reach the target of your actions?

What prevented you from doing more?

Did you have sufficient means (finances, time, material, psychological)?

What do you want to reach by succeeding in your goals?

How much time do you think you need to reach your goal (it's important to set a deadline in order to keep yourself in the reality of the means you need)?

What are the signs which will definitely prove that the actions you are planning to undertake were appropriate?

When will you know for sure that you have reached your goal?

What have you understood about the situation of this function compared to others? What did you decide?

What would be for you the most satisfying way of reaching your new goal?

What will be the impact of your success in reaching this goal for the people around you?

What are the necessary changes that you need to do in order to reach your goal?

What type of support do you need? Who should support you?

How will you get that support?

What is the first step you could take to go in this direction?

I want to tell a tale about my birth, a touch of my childhood...

At the beginning I was a seed... and my name is...

I was born on the:

In this hospital:

At that time:

My weight:

My size:

My eyes were:

My hair was:

My particularity:

Apparently my birth was:

I remember that as a baby I used to:

If I could speak to the baby I used to be, I would say:

If I could speak as the baby I used to be, I would say:

I was breastfed...I loved baby bottles... I had a dummy... I used to suck my thumb...

I was told that I looked like...

People used to say that I was rather a baby that ...

There is a picture which touches me: ...

If I don't have any picture I can imagine myself as a baby that rather...

I arrived (first, second...) I am the brother/sister of ...

I can remember a teddy bear, a doll, a sheet, a pillow...

I can remember the games and toys...

I can remember the story time...

I can remember the moments we lived and shared...

I can remember particular smells, perfumes, colours, sounds...

When I was a child, I had secrets... I have always kept them by the way...

The earliest I can remember was when I was...

I can remember that I used to be kept by my baby sitter:...

I can remember and still see the place I was born in, the place where I spent my childhood...

The year and the day I was born in I know the following happened on Earth:...

The gift within me is...

When I was a baby I used to be scared of...

When I was a child I used to be scared of...

As a baby I needed...

As a child I needed...

As a baby I was able to...

As a child I was able to...

As a baby I used to dream of...

As a child I used to dream of...

As a baby I used to love...

As a child I used to love...

My health as a baby...

My health as a child...

I starting speaking at the age of...

I started walking at the age of...

My first teeth came out at the age of...

As a baby I already knewahow to...

As a child I already knew how to...

For me birth means...

For me rebirth means...

For me knowing myself means...

For me getting to know myself again means...

GLOSSARY:

Al Hamdulillah: All praise is to God.

Allahu akbar: God Is The Greatest.

Asr (Salah): The prayer in the middle of the afternoon.

Assalamu alaykum: May peace be on you.

Benti: My daughter.

Dhikr: Remembrance of God, it is also one of the names of the Quran.

Dhuha (Salah): Voluntary prayer made after the sunrise.

Duhr (Salah): Prayer at the beginning of the afternoon.

Fitra: Original predisposition to faith in God or first form of Islam.

Hadith: Words of the Prophet (peace and blessings be upon him).

Haram: Sacred space in which the Kaaba is located.

Ihram: Sacral clothing made of two pieces of white cloth.

Isha (Salah): Prayer in the evening.

Kaaba: Cubical building built by the Prophets Ibrahim and Ismail representing the sacred house of God located in Mekka.

Kheyr: Goodness, expression to show hope.

Kiswa: Black cloth embroidered with gold and silver threads that covers the Kaaba.

Maghreb (Salah): Prayer after the sun went down.

Masha Allah: Literally, what God wants, words pronounced as a form of exclamation in front of divine creating and greatness, an event or something inspiring, showing astonishment, etc.

Miqat: Point drawing the sacred space surrounding the Kaaba, from which every pilgrim will have to wear the Ihram or the sacral clothing.

Omra: The lesser pilgrimage essentially consisting in visiting the sacred house of God.

Qudussi: Of divine origin.

Rabbi: My God, my Lord, my Teacher.

Rajab: Seventh month in the lunar calendar.

Seerat: Bridge, as thin as a hair and as sharp as a blade crossing Hellfire and which every single human being will have to cross.

Seerat (Al mustaqim): The straight path.

Shahada: Testimony that there is no God but Allah and that Muhammad is His Messenger and the last of the prophets.

Subh (Salah): Voluntary prayer before Fajr Salah.

SubhanAllah: Glory be to God free of any fault.

Talbiya: Words of the pilgrims replying to the call to pilgrimage sent by the Prophet Ibrahim.

Wird: Spiritual daily programme consisting in duas, Quran and remembrance of God in order to educate the spirit and elevate the soul.

TESTIMONIALS:

Before publishing this book its content has been tested on an audience of thirty people around meetings over six months, inviting the participants to a personal and spiritual quest through the chapters of this book. Below are their testimonials:

Laure M.: "Interesting and fulfilling training... It helped me to stand back from my life and take it back into my own hands."

Fatima L.: "I registered to the training not really knowing what I was looking for, I was in a blurry moment of my life and couldn't define where this unrest came from. Things weren't going well but I couldn't find the reasons for this. In the first class during the training I understood that before looking for answers I had to find the questions. My first relief was discovering the WHY before the HOW. I understood that I wasn't a being which was split into different parts, I was part of a social network, of my family, of my friends group. I had never seen things through this perspective. For me, I was the only reason for my problems and was the only one able to solve them.

I also had to reconcile myself with myself, in other words to look at myself without any hostility nor guilt, and start looking at myself with goodwill. We really think that we know ourselves that when we discover ourselves under a new light, we are really unsettled. That's how I feel about this training: a real destabilising effect. There are many questions and I sometimes felt powerless in front of some of these questions: some words echoed in me, others didn't make sense to met yet. Session after session, we managed to build an atmosphere of trust and I understood that the testimonials of sufferings and the experiences that others had were also part of the quest for myself. After these few weeks, the work to do on myself is still huge, I need to answer thousands of questions, time is lacking and the introspection is sometimes unpleasant sometimes even painful but at least I am sure of one thing, I took the right train."

Nassira N.: "This training was the source of little destabilising moments for me. This forced me to look back at my life, why I am here now and where I am heading to. The idea of this novel in which the principal character can be anyone of us really helped me put words on my pains. I understood that eventually the most important is not what happens to us but how we react to it. We learn how to relativise. These different steps help us evolve towards a better understanding of ourselves. In the end, we learn that life is: a path to faith, steps, projects and one goal which is to come closer to God. I would recommend this training to all those who want to be accompanied in order to race towards their mission, thriving and without any complex. I was really happy to see such a project within our community. May Allah reward you Myriam."

COMING SOON IN ENGLISH:

Once Upon A Time, A Man And A Woman
They Got Married And Were Very Surprised
Which Relationship Do You Want To Build?